OUR BROAD PRESENT

Insurrections: Critical Studies in Religion, Politics, and Culture

Insurrections: Critical Studies in Religion, Politics, and Culture

Slavoj Žižek, Clayton Crockett, Creston Davis, Jeffrey W. Robbins, Editors

The intersection of religion, politics, and culture is one of the most discussed areas in theory today. It also has the deepest and most wide-ranging impact on the world. Insurrections: Critical Studies in Religion, Politics, and Culture will bring the tools of philosophy and critical theory to the political implications of the religious turn. The series will address a range of religious traditions and political viewpoints in the United States, Europe, and other parts of the world. Without advocating any specific religious or theological stance, the series aims nonetheless to be faithful to the radical emancipatory potential of religion.

Series page continued on page 91

OUR BROAD PRESENT

Time and Contemporary Culture

Hans Ulrich Gumbrecht

COLUMBIA UNIVERSITY PRESS

NEW YORK

COLUMBIA UNIVERSITY PRESS

PUBLISHERS SINCE 1893

New York   Chichester, West Sussex

cup.columbia.edu

Copyright © 2011 Suhrkamp Verlag

Copyright © 2014 Columbia University Press

All rights reserved

Library of Congress Cataloging-in-Publication Data

Gumbrecht, Hans Ulrich.

Our broad present: time and contemporary culture / Hans Ulrich Gumbrecht.

pages cm.—(Insurrections: critical studies in religion, politics, and culture)

Includes bibliographical references and index.

ISBN 978-0-231-16360-6 (cloth: alk. paper)—ISBN 978-0-231-16361-3

(pbk.: alk. paper)—ISBN 978-0-231-53761-2 (e-book)

1. Space and time.   2. Civilization, Modern—21st century.   I. Title.

BD632.G86 2014

190—dc23

2013041364

CONTENTS

ACKNOWLEDGMENTS

Chapter 2 previously appeared as "A Negative Anthropology of Globalization" in Francisco González, ed., *The Multiple Faces of Globalization* (Madrid: BBVA, 2009), pp. 230–241; chapter 3 previously appeared as "Stagnation" in *Merkur: Deutsche Zeitschrift für europäisches Denken* 712/713 (Berlin: Klett-Cotta, 2008), pp. 876–885; chapter 4 previously appeared as "Lost in Focused Intensity: Spectator Sports and Strategies of Re-Enchantment" in Joshua Landy and Michael Saler, eds., *The Re-Enchantment of the World: Secular Magic in a Rational Age* (Stanford: Stanford University Press, 2009), pp. 149–158; chapter 5 previously appeared as "Warum wir Klassiker brauchen. Ideengeschichten aus dem Kalten Krieg" in *Zeitschrift für Ideengeschichte* (Munich: Beck, 2010), pp. 111–112; chapter 6 previously appeared as "Infinite Availability: About Hyper-Communication (and Old Age)" in Ulrik Ekman, ed., *Throughout: Art and Culture Emerging with Ubiquitous Computing* (Cambridge: MIT Press, 2012), English republication in Timothy Kuhn, ed., *Matters of Communication: Political, Cultural, and Technological Challenges to Communication Theorizing* (New York: Hampton, 2011), pp. 13–22. "Tracking a Hypothesis"; chapter 3, "Stagnation: Temporal, Intellectual, Heavenly"; and "In the Broad Present" have been translated from the German by Henry Erik Butler.

TRACKING A HYPOTHESIS

A rather famous colleague of mine (recently retired), whose books, arguments, and intellectual elegance I have admired ever since beginning my academic career, often says of himself, with seeming modesty, that, in all his life, he has had "only one good idea." Then, after an artful pause to gauge the effect of his words, he changes his meaning by adding that this is hardly so serious a matter, since "most people don't even have that much." Here I would like to follow the example of the aforementioned party, whose name is Hayden White. In a good forty years of research and writing, my one idea (which has, I hope, had some impact) has taken the form of a hardheaded insistence that the things-of-the-world, however we encounter them, also possess a dimension of presence. This is the case despite our quotidian and scholarly focus on interpretation and meaning—and even if we almost always overlook the dimension of presence in our culture.

By "presence" I have meant—and still mean—that things inevitably stand at a distance from or in proximity to our bodies; whether they "touch" us directly or not, they have substance. I addressed this state of affairs in *Production of Presence*, which appeared in German as *Diesseits der Hermeneutik*. The book received this title—which may be rendered *Hermeneutics of This World*—because it is my impression that the dimension of presence might deserve a position of priority relative to the praxis of interpretation, which ascribes meaning to an object. This is not the case because presence is "more important" than the operations of consciousness and intention, but rather because, perhaps, it is "more elementary." At the same time, the German title betrays something resembling the mild oedipal revolt of a man already over fifty. Relegating interpretation and hermeneutics to a restricted academic terrain (so to speak) was my small—and perhaps even petty—revenge against an overwhelming tradition of intellectual "depth," which I had found embodied in some heroes of profundity among my academic "fathers." Because of my background and (dis)inclinations, I had never felt entirely adequate to such depth.

Almost naturally—should, indeed, this be possible in the intellectual world—and without any particular programmatic objective, my intuition of presence developed in three directions. *In 1926: Living on the Edge of Time*, which preceded *Production of Presence*, I had asked what consequences attention to the dimension of presence might hold for our relationship to the past. An essay on the beauty of athletics addressed the same question with regard to aesthetic experience. Finally, in *The Powers of Philology* I tried to show that the dimension of presence invariably factors into encounters of a textual kind.

Afterward—and I still have not abandoned this hopeful ambition entirely—I wanted to see if I would enjoy the good fortune of striking upon a second idea. (In this I was prompted by Jorge Luis Borges and imagined that what is intellectually decisive does not consist of "discovering" or "producing" ideas so much as "stumbling upon" and "grasping for" them—intercepting ideas and giving them form.) Unfortunately, I have not yet "caught" a second idea, and all the projects I have pursued in recent years are clear extensions of my intuition concerning presence. I have attempted to describe *Stimmung*, the relationship we entertain with our environment, as a presence-phenomenon—the "lightest touch that occurs when the material world surrounding us affects the surface of our bodies." At the moment, I am working on a book about the decade following the Second World War because I believe that in this period a form of "latency" predominated—a presence, to be understood as a kind of "stowaway," that can produce effects and radiate energy while escaping efforts to identify and apprehend it.

After the books on presence had appeared, friends whose opinions I take very seriously surprised me by urging me to reflect systematically on, and write about, the existential and, indeed, the ethical consequences of these publications. The task, I suspect, would have demanded too much of me—or did I, half-consciously, feign modesty only to hide a visceral disinclination to "ethics" and other kinds of prescriptive "self-help" literature? At any rate, my reservations were hardly consistent. As attested by the chapters of the book at hand (to say nothing of other works), I have gladly been induced, time and again, to analyze contemporary social and cultural phenomena from the perspective of presence—or at least to sketch out the lines such an inquiry might assume. There were occasions and exhortations to do so behind every part of this book, even if I always sought a way out by pleading an utter lack of competency or adducing some other reason. It is both an obligation for, and a privilege of, humanists to practice "risky thinking." That is to say, instead of subordinating ourselves to rational schemes of evidence and the constraints of systems, we "scientists of the mind" (*Geisteswissenschaftler*) should seek to confront and imagine whatever might entail a disruption of everyday life and the assumptions underlying its functions. To take a basic example: no one can simply "get away" from the rhythms and structures that constitute our globalized present and its forms of communication; yet, at the same time, it is important to hold firm to the possibility of doing so inasmuch as it provides an alternative to what is only too readily accepted as "normal."

The five chapters comprising the book at hand have a superficial—which is not to say inconsequential—point of convergence with the contemporary world insofar as they came about when, accepting requests from others, I justified and excused what I subsequently wrote as instances of intellectual risk taking. Later, favorably inclined readers discovered—and, through their observations, I did too—that another plane of convergence existed where the analyses and arguments of the chapters connected, yielding a complex and contoured diagnosis of the present. The complementarity and coherence that were evident a posteriori are due, evidently, to the fact that each part of the book proceeds by taking up two chains of thought that are very different in origin and tonality. The first is the thesis (inspired by Michel Foucault and Niklas Luhmann) that the emergence of second-order observation has shaped the epistemological framework of Western culture since the early nineteenth century. Reinhart Koselleck dubbed the period between 1780 and 1830 the *Sattelzeit* ("saddle time" or "saddle period"); from then on, self-reflexive thought became the habitus of intellectuals, synonymous with thought itself.

But if, on the one hand, I sought to contextualize my account and analysis of the present day in terms of the consequences attending institutionalized second-order observation in 1800, I also yielded, time and again, to the temptation to impart, to the history of epistemology, a resonance that comes from the tradition of cultural criticism. Perhaps this melancholy tone was first heard in the early materialism of the seventeenth century, inasmuch as it represented the existential (and never really "political") protest against a culture that, in a more and more one-sided fashion, posited a transcendental foundation for the structure and functions of human consciousness—a development accompanied by the thinning of concrete corporality as the substrate of human life. Today—when, for most people, the everyday occurs as a fusion of consciousness and software—this process has reached levels that can hardly be surpassed. I place emphasis on a culturally critical mood because here my thinking meets up with attempts by others to describe our present, even if, at the same time, it also differs from them. Under headings such as "biopolitics," "body politics," and "ecocriticism," the human body—and with it, the things-of-the-world—are now receiving renewed attention and interest. For me, too, this is a point where multiple trajectories converge. The observations of my contemporaries almost always involve a critique of the present situation and suggestions for changing it. Owing, however, to a fundamental skepticism about the possibility of directing events—or even changing them in part—I prefer to retain a cautious distance. I believe that the situations faced today represent a continuation of human evolution "by cultural means." For this reason—and notwithstanding appearances to the contrary—they lie entirely outside what we can hope to control.

An intellectual framework for the analysis of the present results where the history of epistemology that followed upon the emergence of second-order observation intersects with cultural criticism of the melancholy sort. In part, the chapters of the book presuppose this convergence; in part, they elaborate it. Central to this framework is the idea that the configuration of time that developed in the early nineteenth century has, for about half a century now (and with effects that become clearer every day), been succeeded by another configuration for which no name as yet exists. The title conferred upon the now obsolete chronotope—"historical thought/consciousness"—bears witness to the fact that it was once institutionalized so broadly and thoroughly that it could be mistaken for time *tout court*. It is Koselleck's lasting achievement to have historicized, against this tendency, "historical consciousness" itself. To provide a background and contrast for the chronotope governing our own time, I would like to refer, in six points, to features of the historical mindset that Koselleck describes.

First, "historically conscious" mankind imagines itself on a linear path moving through time (therefore, it is not time itself that moves, as occurs in other chronotopes). Second, "historical thought" presumes that all phenomena are affected by change in time—time appears, that is, as an absolute agent of transformation. Third, as mankind moves along in time, it thinks it has left the past behind; the distance afforded by the present moment depreciates the value of past experiences as points of orientation. Fourth, the future presents itself as an open horizon of possibilities toward which humanity is making its way. Between the future and the past—and this is point five—the present narrows to a "brief, no-longer-perceptible moment of transition" (in the words of Baudelaire). It is my belief—point six—that the constricted present of this "history" came to provide the Cartesian subject with its epistemological habitat. Here was the site where the subject, adapting experiences from the past to the present and the future, made choices among the possibilities the latter offered. Picking options from what the future holds is the basis of—and frame for—what we call agency (*Handeln*).

Still today, we reproduce the topic of "historical time" in everyday conversation, as well as in intellectual and academic discourses, even if it no longer provides the basis for the ways we acquire experiences or act. That we no longer live in historical time can be seen most clearly with respect to the future. For us, the future no longer presents itself as an open horizon of possibilities; instead, it is a dimension increasingly closed to all prognoses—and which, at the same time, seems to draw near as a menace. Global warming will proceed with all the consequences that have been foreseen for quite some time; the question remains whether humanity will manage to accrue sufficient credit for a few additional years before the most catastrophic consequences of the situation arrive. Despite all the talk about how the past has supposedly gone missing, another problem the new chronotope presents is that we are no longer able to bequeath anything to posterity. Instead of ceasing to provide points of orientation, *pasts* flood our present; automated, electronic systems of memory play a central role in the process. Between the pasts that engulf us and the menacing future, the present has turned into a dimension of expanding simultaneities. All the pasts of recent memory form part of this spreading present; it is increasingly difficult for us to exclude any kind of fashion or music that originated in recent decades from the time now. The broad present, with its concurrent worlds, has, always and already, offered too many possibilities; therefore, the identity it possesses—if it has one at all—lacks clear contours. At the same time, the closure of futurity (at least in the strict sense) makes it impossible to act, since no action can occur where no place exists for its realization to be projected. The expanding present offers room to move toward the future and the past, yet such efforts seem ultimately to return to their point of departure. Here they produce the impression of intransitive "mobilization" (to borrow a metaphor from Lyotard). Such unmoving motion often reveals itself to be stagnant, the end of directed purpose. If, then, the narrow present of "history" was the epistemological habitat of the Cartesian subject, another figure of reference (and self-reference) must emerge in the broad present. Might the foregoing explain why we, for a few years now, have felt the intellectual pressure—which has only grown more intense—to make, once again, aspects of its *physis* part of the way we envision and conceptualize human beings?

In our present, the epistemological disposition to fashion a figure of self-reference that is more strongly rooted in the body and in space meets up with a yearning that emerged in reaction to a world determined by excessive emphasis on consciousness; this is the yearning that, as we have noted, found its tone and expression in the melancholy strain of cultural criticism. Within the new, expansive present, then, there are always already two dynamics pulling apart and, at the same time, forming a field of tension. On one side lies an insistence on concreteness, corporality, and the presence of human life, where the echo of cultural criticism merges with the effects of the new chronotope. Such an insistence stands opposed to radical spiritualization, which abstracts from space, the body, and sensory contact with the things-of-the-world—this is the "disenchantment" entailed by the "process of modernization." Between these two powerful vectors, our new present has begun to unfold its particular form and to command a unique fascination.

I have often heard the criticism or objection that I clearly, and even nostalgically, side with presence and the senses against the cultural achievements of consciousness, abstraction, and, finally, electronic technology. Such observations are certainly accurate, and I do not care to defend myself against them. It seems unnecessary to do so, above all because I in no way seek to make a normative claim for my choices. Yet I would certainly appeal to the rights of age—an age that advances in years—that I be allowed to preserve some distance, and even a polemical distance, from the developments of recent times. I am sure that the electronic world, its rhythm and its forms of communication, are repugnant to me and difficult to accept because they began their march at a moment when I—at some forty years of age—had found certain arrangements in my everyday life and work that made me feel comfortable and productive. Many of them—for example, writing long notes on white index cards with a soft surface or dictating correspondence on a small tape recorder—today seem like islands of activity threatened by an electronic flood that will never recede.

The future of our increasingly warm planet transforms into a vision I have of a technological present, long since past, that extends into our broad present. Don't those of us who are older have the right to remain on our islands for as long as possible? Why should we clumsily adapt to the demands of the electronic that dominate the new present? We are already living in a vast moment of simultaneities. There is no need to reject us—we who embody one of many pasts—from our havens in the broad present.

OUR BROAD PRESENT

I. PRESENCE IN LANGUAGE OR PRESENCE ACHIEVED AGAINST LANGUAGE?

"From Language to Logic—and Back," the title of Ruediger Bubner's opening lecture for the Hegel Congress 2005, had a structural similarity to the movement that I propose (and have been invited to) to pursue here. I will start out from language and try to reach something that is not language; then I want to return to language from that something which is not language. Instead of "language," however, that which is not language, in my essay, will be what I have come to call presence.

I will divide the presentation of this simple back-and-forth movement into three parts. The first part contains four premises that will lead us from language to presence:[1] they are the briefest possible explanation of what I resent and criticize within the hermeneutic tradition (a), which critique will make transparent my conceptions of "metaphysics" and of a "critique of metaphysics" (b). These notions will justify my use of the word *presence* (c) and the typological distinction that I propose to make between "presence culture" and "meaning culture" (d). The second part of my brief reflection will trace a way back (or a variety of ways back) from presence to language by describing six modes through which presence can exist in language or, in other words, six modes through which presence and language can become amalgamated (the metaphor of amalgamation points to a principally difficult, rather than natural, relationship between presence and language). These modes are language as presence, presence in philological work, language that can trigger aesthetic experience, the language of mystic experience, the openness of language toward the world, and literature as epiphany. In the third, retrospective part I will ask whether these six types of amalgamation between presence and language have led us to a horizon of questions and problems similar to the one that Martin Heidegger tried to address when, in the later stages of his philosophy, he was using, with ever growing insistence, the metaphorical evocation of language as "the house of Being."

1

When my colleagues, the literary critics and literary theorists, speak of "language," they normally think of something that requires "interpretation," something that invites us to attribute well-circumscribed meanings to words. Like some other literary critics and, I believe, even more philosophers of my generation (among whom Jean-Luc Nancy may be the most outspoken),[2] I have grown weary of this intellectual one-way traffic as it has been based on and upheld by a certain, narrow, and yet totalizing understanding of hermeneutics. I also have long experienced the absolutism of all postlinguistic-turn varieties of philosophy as intellectually limiting and I have not found much consolation in what I like to characterize as the "linguistic existentialism" of deconstruction, i.e., the sustained complaint and melancholia (in its endless variations) about the alleged incapacity of language to refer to the things of the world. Should it really be the core function of literature, in all its different forms and tones, to draw its readers' attention, over and again, to the all too familiar view that language cannot refer, as Paul de Man seemed to claim whenever he wrote about the "allegory of reading"?

These are, in hopefully convenient condensation, the main feelings and reasons that made me become part of yet another movement within the humanities that has a (perhaps even well-deserved) reputation of being "worn out." I am referring to the "critique of Western metaphysics." At least I can claim that the way in which I use the word *metaphysics* is more elementary than and therefore different from its dominant meanings in contemporary philosophy. When I say metaphysics, I want to activate the word's literal meaning of something "beyond the merely physical." I want to point to an intellectual style (prevailing in the humanities today) that only allows for one gesture, and one type of operation, and that is the operation of "going beyond" what is regarded to be a "merely physical surface" and of thus finding, "beyond or below the merely physical surface," that which is supposed to really matter, i.e., a meaning (which, in order to underline its distance from the surface, is often called profound).

My departure from metaphysics in this very sense takes into account and insists on the experience that our relationship to things (and to cultural artifacts in specific) is, inevitably, never only a relationship of meaning attribution. As long as I use the word *things* to refer to what the Cartesian tradition calls *res extensae*, we also and always live in and are aware of a spatial relationship to these things. Things can be "present" or "absent" to us, and, if they are present, they are either closer to or further away from our bodies. By calling them present, then, in the very original sense of Latin *prae-esse*, we are saying that things are "in front" of ourselves and thereby tangible. There are no further implications that I propose to associate with this concept.

Based on the historical observation, however, that certain cultures, like our own "modern" culture, for example (whatever we exactly may mean by *modern*), have a greater tendency than other cultures to bracket the dimension of presence and its implications, I have come to propose a typology (in the traditional Weberian sense) between "meaning cultures" and "presence cultures." Here are a few of the (inevitably, and without any bad conscience, "binary") distinctions that I propose to make.[3] In a meaning culture, firstly, the dominant form of human self-reference will always correspond to the basic outline of what Western culture calls subject and subjectivity, i.e., it will refer to a body-less observer who, from a position of eccentricity vis-à-vis the world of things, will attribute meanings to those things. A presence culture, in contrast, will integrate both spiritual and physical existence into its human self-reference (think, as an illustration, of the motif of the "spiritual and bodily resurrection from the dead" in medieval Christianity). It follows from this initial distinction that, secondly, in a presence culture humans consider themselves to be part of the world of objects instead of being ontologically separated from it (this may have been the view that Heidegger wanted to recover with "being-in-the-world" as one of his key concepts in *Being and Time*). Thirdly, and on a higher level of complexity, human existence, in a meaning culture, unfolds and realizes itself in constant and ongoing attempts at transforming the world ("actions") that are based on the interpretation of things and on the projection of human desires into the future. This drive toward change and transformation is absent from presence cultures where humans just want to inscribe their behavior into what they consider to be structures and rules of a given cosmology (what we call rituals are frames for such attempts to correspond to cosmological frames).

I will abandon this typology here, for I trust that it has fulfilled the function that I have assigned to it within the larger context of my argument: I wanted to illustrate that, on the one hand, language in meaning cultures does cover all those functions that modern philosophy of European descent is presupposing and talking about. On the other hand, it is much less obvious what roles language can play in presence cultures (or in a world seen from a presence culture perspective). The six types of "amalgamations" between language and presence that I want to refer to in the second section of my text are intended to present a multifaceted answer to this same question.

2

The first paradigm is *language, above all spoken language, as a physical reality*, and it highlights the aspect in relation to which Hans-Georg Gadamer spoke of the "volume" of language, in distinction to its propositional or apophantic content.[4] "As a physical reality, spoken language not only touches and affects our acoustic sense, but our bodies in their entirety." We thus perceive language, in the least invasive way, i.e., quite literally, as the light touch of sound on our skin, even if we cannot understand what its words are supposed to mean. Such perceptions can well be pleasant and even desirable—and in this sense we all know how one can grasp certain qualities of poetry in a reading without knowing the language that is being used. As soon as the physical reality of language has a form, a form that needs to be achieved against its status of being a time object in the sense proper ("ein Zeitobjekt im eigentlichen Sinn," according to Husserl's terminology), we will say that it has a "rhythm"—a rhythm that we can feel and identify independently of the meaning language "carries."[5] Language as a physical reality that has form, i.e., rhythmic language, will fulfill a number of specific functions. It can coordinate the movements of individual bodies; it can support the performance of our memory (think of those rhymes through which we used to learn some basic rules of Latin grammar); and, by supposedly lowering the level of our alertness, it can have (as Nietzsche said) an "intoxicating" effect. Certain presence cultures even attribute an incantatory function to rhythmic language, i.e., the capacity of making absent things present and present things absent (this indeed was the expectation associated with medieval charms).[6]

A second, very different type of amalgamation between presence and language lies in the *basic practices of philology* (in their original function as text curatorship). In a short recent book, I have argued that—much counter to his traditional image—the philologist's activities are preconsciously driven by very primary desires that we can describe as desires for (full) presence (and I understand that a desire for "full presence" is a desire without the possibility of fulfillment—which precisely makes it a desire from a Lacanian point of view).[7] Collecting textual fragments, in this sense, would presuppose a deeply repressed wish of quite literally eating what remains of ancient papyri or medieval manuscripts. A wish to incorporate the texts in question (to play them like an actor) might underlie the passion for producing historical editions (in all of their various philological styles)—think of an act as basic as "sounding out" a Goethe poem and discovering that it will only rhyme if you pronounce it with a (more than slight) Frankfurt accent. As they "fill up" the margins of handwritten and printed pages, erudite commentaries, finally, may relate to a physical wish for plenitude and exuberance. It would probably be very difficult (if not impossible) to disentangle, in all detail, such cases of intertwinedness between presence drives and scholarly ambitions. But what matters to me, in this context, is the intuition that they do converge, much more than we normally imagine, in many forms of philological work.

If you follow, as I tend to do, at least regarding present-day Western culture, Niklas Luhmann's suggestion for a characterization of aesthetic experience (Luhmann, within the parameters of his philosophy, tried to describe what was specific about "communication" within the "art system" as a social system), then *any kind of language that is capable of triggering aesthetic experience* will appear as a third case of the amalgamation between presence and language. Communication in the art system, for Luhmann, is the one form of communication within which (purely sensual) perception is not only a presupposition but a content carried, together with meaning, by language. This description corresponds to an experience of poems (or of literary prose rhythms) as drawing our attention to those physical aspects of language (and their possible forms) that we tend to bracket otherwise. Contrary to a long prevailing (and still dominating) opinion in literary studies, however, I do not believe that the different dimensions of poetic form (i.e. rhythm, rhyme, stanzas, etc.) function in ways that subordinate them to the dimension of meaning (for example, as the so-called theory of poetic overdetermination suggests, by giving stronger contours to complex semantic configurations). Rather, I see poetic forms engaging in an oscillation with meaning, in the sense that a reader/listener of poetry can never pay full attention to both sides. This, I think, is the reason why a cultural prescription in Argentina excludes the dancing of a tango whenever the tango has lyrics. For the choreography of tango as a dance, with its asymmetry between male and female steps, against which harmony needs to be achieved at every moment, is so demanding that it requires full attention for the music—which state would inevitably be reduced by the interference of a text that would divert part of this attention.

Mystical experience and the language of mysticism is my fourth paradigm. By constantly referring to its own incapacity of rendering the intense presence of the divine, mystical language produces the paradoxical effect of stimulating imaginations that seem to make this very presence palpable. In the description of her visions, Saint Teresa de Avila, for example, uses highly erotic images under the permanent condition of an "as if." The encounter with Jesus, for her, is "as if being penetrated by a sword," and at the same time she feels "as if an angel was emerging from her body." Rather than taking these forms of expression literally, however, as the description of something, i.e., of a mystical experience that truly exceeds the limits of language, a both secular and analytic view will understand mystical experience itself as an effect of language and of its inherent powers of self-persuasion.

Yet another mode of amalgamation can be described as *language being open toward the world of things*. It includes texts that switch from the semiotic paradigm of representation to a deictic attitude where words are experienced as pointing to things rather than standing "for them." Nouns then turn into names because they seem to skip the always totalizing dimension of concepts and become individually attached, temporarily at least, with individual objects. Francis Ponge's thing-poems use and cultivate this potential of language. I recently had a similar impression when I was reading an autobiographical sketch by the great physicist Erwin Schroedinger,[8] whose obsession with descriptive preciseness seems to have rejected the effect of abstraction that is inherent to all concepts. Nouns therefore seem attached to individual objects in Schroedinger's text and thus begin to function like names, producing a textual impression that is strangely reminiscent of medieval charms. In a different way, certain passages in Louis-Ferdinand Céline's novels seem to be specifically open to the world of objects. There the rhythm of the prose copies the rhythm of movements or of events to be evoked and thus establishes an analogic relationship to these movements and events that also bypasses the digital principle of representation. If texts like Ponge's poems or Schroedinger's autobiographical sketch seem to reach toward things in space, Céline's texts appear open to be affected by and resonate with things.

Finally, whoever is familiar with the twentieth-century tradition of high modernism knows the claim, central, above all, for the work of James Joyce, that *literature can be the place of epiphany* (a more skeptical description would once again rather speak of the capacity of literature to produce "effects of epiphany"). In its theological usage the concept of epiphany refers to the appearance of a thing, of a thing that requires space, a thing that is either absent or present.

For a conception of language that concentrates exclusively on the dimension of meaning, epiphanies, in this very literal sense, and texts must be separated by a relation of heteronomy. But if we take into account, as I have suggested throughout this series of examples, the phenomenology of language as a physical reality and, with it, the incantatory potential of language, then a convergence between literature and epiphany seems to be much less outlandish. To concede that such moments of epiphany do occur, but do so under the specific temporal conditions that Karl Heinz Bohrer has characterized as those of "suddenness" and "irreversible departure,"[9] may be a contemporary way of mediating between our desire for epiphanies and a modern skepticism that this desire cannot completely outdo.

3

Passing through six modes of amalgamation between language and presence, we have covered the distance between two extremes that the title of my essay tries to pinpoint. We started out by drawing attention to the always given but, within modern culture, systematically overlooked or even bracketed physical presence of language and we have arrived at the claim that language can produce epiphanies, which claim evokes an exceptional situation and achievement that has to be wrested, so to speak, from and even against the grain of the normal functioning of language. Certainly, in the growing complexity of our different paradigms, the different relations between language and presence do not obey the structural model of the "metaphysical" two-leveledness that distinguishes between "material surface" and "semantic depth," between "negligible foreground" and "meaningful background." But what could then be an alternative model that allows us to think through the rather tense harmonious oscillations between language and presence in their variety?

Given that I believe in a convergence between Heidegger's concept of Being and the notion of presence that I have been using here,[10] I do indeed see a promise in his description of "language as the house of Being," a promise, however, whose redemption may well end up departing from what Heidegger meant to mean with these words. There are four aspects of his metaphor that I am specifically interested in. Counter to its current understanding, I want to highlight, in the first place, that a house makes, more often, those who live in it less invisible than visible. In this very sense, language is not so much a window, not the expression of the presence with which it can be intertwined. Nevertheless, and secondly, we take a house to be the promise (if not the guarantee) for the close-ness of those who inhabit it. Think, for example, of the language of mysticism. It may not make the divine fully present and it is certainly not an expression of the divine. But, in reading mystical texts, some of us feel that they approach the divine. What I appreciate, thirdly and above all, about the metaphor of "lan-guage as the house of Being" is its spatial denotation. Different from the clas-sical hermeneutic paradigm of "expression,"[11] and its standard implication that whatever will be expressed has to be purely spiritual, seeing language as "the house of Being" (or as the house of presence) makes us imagine that which inhabits the house as having "volume" and thereby sharing the ontological sta-tus of things.

This does not imply, however, that I understand Heidegger's concept of Being as a—perhaps slightly embarrassed—return of the *Ding an sich*. Rather, I hold that the concept of Being points to a relationship between things and *Dasein* in which *Dasein* does no longer conceive of itself as eccentric, as onto-logically separated from the things and their dimension. Instead of cutting off our rapport to the things, as the "linguistic turn" had proposed we do, "language as the house of Being," language in its multiple tension-filled convergences with presence, would then be, finally, a medium in and through which we can hope for a reconciliation between *Dasein* and the objects of the world.

Is it realistic at all (or simply illusory) to assume that such a reconciliation between *Dasein* and objects might ever occur? I do not feel confident enough to try and answer this question. But it is worth thinking about the fact that, in the contemporary cultural situation, I am far from being the only intellectual who asks such a question,[12] a question that, only a few years ago, must have looked so utterly naive that nobody dared to ask it. Now longing to recuperate an existential closeness to the dimension of things may well be a reaction to our contemporary everyday. More than ever before, it has turned into an everyday of only virtual realities, into an everyday where modern communication tech-nologies have given us omnipresence and have thus eliminated space from our existence, into an everyday where the real presence of the world has shrunk into a presence on the screen—of which development the new wave of "reality shows" is but the most tautological and hyperbolically helpless symptom.[13]

For those among us who hold the positions of the linguistic turn to be an ultimate philosophical wisdom, this desire for the presence of the world must appear to be a desire against better philosophical insight. But the lack of belief in the possibility of a desire beingfulfilled of course does not imply that it will necessarily disappear sooner or later (even less implying that such a desire is pointless). What then could be a viable relation to language for those who find implausible what I believe, namely that language may become (again?) the medium of reconciliation with the things of the world? The answer is that they may still use language to point to and even to praise those forms of experience that keep our desire for presence alive. Which, of course, suggests that it is better to suffer from an unfulfilled desire than to lose desire altogether.

II. A NEGATIVE ANTHROPOLOGY
OF GLOBALIZATION

1

Ouro Preto, in the Brazilian state of Minas Gerais, far away from the Atlantic coast, is a well-preserved baroque town with a bit less than a hundred thousand inhabitants today—but it may well have been the wealthiest and most powerful city on the American continent around 1700 when, under the name of Vila Rica, it provided the Portuguese crown with gold and precious stones. Despite a steady flow of tourists with historical interests, Ouro Preto cannot be reached by air or by train, which adds to the impression that it is a place far away from the present. About fifteen kilometers away lies Mariana, a smaller and also very beautiful (though less spectacular) town that hosts the cathedral of the local diocese and several buildings belonging to the University of Ouro Preto. These buildings were the reason why, on five subsequent late August days, I went five times from my fancy hotel at Ouro Preto to Mariana and back with a car and a driver from the university. Now there is nothing for the die-hard sports fan that I am, especially in Brazil, like talking soccer with professional drivers or conductors—but this driver was different. For when I asked him about his favorite soccer team (expecting that it would be one of the two major league clubs from Belo Horizonte, the state capital), he almost bluntly replied that he did not care about soccer, that the one person in the family who liked sports was his son, whereas his own idol had always been the late Michael Jackson. And my driver went on to speak, with enthusiasm, true compassion, and many details, about Michael Jackson's life and its tragedies, on the road from Ouro Preto to Mariana and back, and he also talked about the innovations that his hero had introduced to the world of show business, about his music and his dancing. By the time we were arriving at Mariana the first time, he even sang—almost without any accent, although he was solidly monolingual—several Michael Jackson hits from many years ago. I, by contrast, Michael Jackson's fellow Californian, just knew his name and that he had recently died and I would certainly not have been able to identify any of his songs all by myself. Thus our conversation was a typical scene of hybridity, as we have come to call it in the age of globalization, a type of scene that often makes conversation difficult because it has knowledge distributed in mutually unexpected ways.[1]

There is, of course, no need to travel to the Brazilian inland or to any other faraway-looking location for whoever wants to experience the effects of globalization.[2] Each time that we sit down in front of our computers to do e-mail, the probably most powerful condition and the certainly most powerful effect of globalization are at our fingertips, quite literally. For, provided that we have the required addresses, the computer makes our colleague next door and an e-mail user, say, in Australia, equidistant for all (or, at least, for most) communicative purposes. It does not take me one fraction of a second more to be present on a computer screen in New Zealand than on the screen of a computer that stands in my own office. Obviously, computers do not give tangibility to the persons whose words and reactions they bring so close, but they can make them visible and audible for us in real time. *Globalization is about information (in the largest possible sense of the word) and the consequences of information transfer being increasingly detached from and independent of specific physical places.*

2

As soon as we mention or even describe effects of globalization, the temptation seems to arise, quite inevitably, of either praising or condemning them. Forty million albums with music from all countries, cultures, and historical periods have now become available to him, my friend Gary told me the other day, thanks to an electronic program that only costs a few dollars per month; how unimaginable that would have been only a few years ago, when he made the transition from collecting records to collecting CDs. Conversely, we intellectuals never miss an opportunity to frown, with august pedagogical responsibility, at the contemporary overflow of opportunities to communicate and at what it has done to shorten the attention span and dry out the fantasies of the younger generations (never, of course, our own fantasies!) or we complain, with a touch of Marxist sourness, about yet another step in the apparently never ending alienation of producers from their products (not to mention the ensuing excesses of economic exploitation). All this critique and all that euphoria just add, endlessly, to the two only and symmetrically opposite attitudes and discourses that have accompanied the different stages of modern culture for centuries, without providing any true analytical power or insight. For that reason I will try to keep my text at a distance from praising globalization or nagging about it. Nor will I engage in any detailed descriptions of globalization phenomena, however worthwhile they may often be, for the simple reason that this has already been done by the globalization specialists of our time.

What I will try to do, instead of praising, criticizing, or analyzing phenomena of globalization, can best be described as bringing together two different but convergent movements of reflection. In the first place, I want to focus on globalization from an existentialist perspective, in other words: I want to understand how globalization typically transforms structures and situations of individual life (rather than writing about its impact on "society," on the "economic system," or on "politics"). I will do so under a premise that has belonged to existentialism since its very beginnings in the first half of the nineteenth century, and that is the assumption that absolute (or divine) norms of what makes an optimal human life and how one can achieve it are not (or perhaps no longer) available to us. The second, complementary, movement of reflection I will explain from a historical angle. Early existentialism turned its central challenge, i.e., the difficulty of believing in a God whose will was hard (if not humanly impossible) to identify, into what we call negative theology, into the paradoxical conception of a divine order wrested from that silent God. In a similar way, I will try to argue along the lines of a "negative anthropology"; I want to speak about some meta-historically and transculturally stable components of human life at a time when an extreme degree of skepticism seems to make such claims unacceptable. In so doing I will rely on my intuition that the process of globalization, by leaving some universal needs and desires of human life unattended, has paradoxically helped to make these needs and desires more visible—because we notice, in our everyday lives, how they remain unsatisfied. So my discussion of globalization is "anthropological" by trying to identify some universal conditions of human existence; and it is "negative" because of the suspicion that some of these structures grow more apparent the less they are in play.[3]

I will now continue to build my argument by describing the contrast between the historically specific future, which not only intellectuals expected to arrive in the mid-twentieth century, and the early twenty-first century present as it has by now established itself (3). On this basis, I will show how globalization can be seen to be an extension of modernity, as the result of its convergence with the Cartesian motif of eliminating the body as a part of human self-reference (4). Modernity and globalization thus imply a tendency to make us independent of the dimension of space. In section 5, I will identify and describe further aspects of globalization in their specific relation to the Cartesian tradition, whereas section (6) will deal with reactions to globalization and how they may enable us to delineate a negative anthropology. In concluding (7), I will point to possible lines of convergence between this argument and other philosophical positions of our time.

3

There is a ride in the oldest of all Disneylands at Anaheim, California, called Futureland that I find to be of particular historical interest, so much so, indeed, that I believe it should be renamed, together with the entire park perhaps, Futureland of the Past—for it beautifully stages the future the world expected to emerge in the mid-1950s, when Disneyland first opened its doors. This ride features small, two-seater cars that leave no freedom of choice or any individual agency to their drivers. Instead, each car is supposed to "find" the way through a relatively complex itinerary of curves, hills, and intersections "all by itself," thus producing an impression of "automatic driving" within a powerful traffic system that takes care of all human needs of movement and locomotion. Such dreams of "automatic" life have always and inevitably implied the imagination of a state that—benignly—overpowers, absorbs, and determines all individual life, much like an optimistic version (it's Disneyland, after all) of Orwell's *1984*. Other rides are inspired—until the present day, and this somehow means counterfactually—by the past utopia of space travel: they give you the illusion of very shaky and at some point even precarious flights to remote galaxies—or the scary impression of fast movements and sharp turns within the absolute darkness of the universe. Lastly, the old Disneyland is filled with leftovers of our former belief in "robots" as more or less humanly shaped machines (their smaller versions tend to look like vacuum cleaners) who were supposed to do all the inferior work that human laziness has always hoped to get rid of—and that the predominantly social-democratic spirit of the twentieth century has declared unworthy of human beings.

Now, I think it is remarkable that none of these three dominant dimensions from the now historical future of the mid-1950s has become either real in our present nor by any means probable for the future we imagine. The overpowering ideas of the "total" state, "total" also in the sense of claiming to take care of the totality of human wishes and needs, the ideas whose hyperbolic version inspired Orwell's novel, have vanished with the demise of the communist governments in Eastern Europe after 1989, regardless of whether one hails or regrets this development. The obvious new and general tendency is a reduction, and even an active withdrawal, of state power as it is reflected by the new concept of "governance," which describes informal orientations for interactive behavior that, rather than being imposed by state law, are emerging between national states and (often multinational) corporations. We might well say that we dispose of much more freedom (we are much more left alone and much less "automatically" guided) than the drivers in Disney's Futureland—and this sometimes confuses us. After all, the navigation systems we so like to use today react very flexibly to our input and even to our errors.

Likewise and even more evidently, our high-flying imagining of space travel and of inhabiting "foreign" planets or perhaps even other galaxies have all but disappeared (and, quite remarkably, they have done so to the same degree that we have stopped worrying about demographic growth). Once again, more definitely perhaps than ever during the past few centuries, the earth defines the limits of our concerns and projects—and this may well be the least frequently mentioned core condition of globalization (which somehow still cultivates a self-image and a rhetoric of aggressive expansion). Collectively and ideologically, we care more about the earth than we used to do when we were still nurturing the dream of leaving it behind ourselves in a spaceship; at the same time and from an individual perspective, the power to cover the planet, quite literally, with our acts of communication has increased exponentially.

Finally, instead of creating battalions of "robots" to do work for us, we have developed, especially during the past three decades, a convergence of our minds with electronic devices, which convergence, rather than a master/slave relationship, looks like an extension and enhancement of our mental (and sometimes even of our physical) efficiency based on a coupling or on a prosthetic integration of our bodies with those electronic machines. Nobody uses electronics without working for himself or herself, and, at the same time, we inevitably also work for others. At first glance, the world of computers produces the impression that we have gained enormous amounts of individual independence and agency—but such a blatantly positive view ignores the addictive nature of these couplings, and it may also belittle the growth of a collective exterior brain that is developing as the accumulated consequence of our computer usage, ending up with more blind power over us than any totalitarian state could ever have programmatically aimed at. For with each e-mail we send, and with each visit to a Web site we make, we add to the complexity and intensity the technical network within which we are communicating, and this means, increasingly, in which we simply exist.

4

It is often said that, at least from the perspective of Western culture, globalization has been coming for at least two centuries now. If we define globalization as growing independence of information from physical space, then a quantitative leap that became quality, both in the sense of going places to acquire specific knowledge and in that of circulating knowledge, happened with the development of railroad networks since the early 1800s. The surge and the new value of the concept "cosmopolitan" was a symptom of this first stage in a long-term development. Its second stage was marked by a series of new communication technologies, starting with the telephone, including the radio, and culminating in television, which medium, after an astonishingly slow start, conquered the entire world within a long decade since the late 1940s. Today, for people who are not very old, it is hard to imagine that Brazilian fans could not watch (*assistir*, as one interestingly says in Brazilian Portuguese) the game in which their team won its first Soccer World Cup against Sweden, in Stockholm in 1958, on TV. The most incisive development, however, although it may well have been the least eventlike stage, was the process of the electronic transformation and socialization of a large (and still rapidly growing) segment of humankind: it enlarged our individual and collective capacity for receiving and circulating information to a hitherto unimaginable degree. A new threshold lying ahead of us, from which we are only separated by legal, not by technological, difficulties, is the Google Project, which promises to make available every document existing on the planet for every computer screen.

    To imagine the realization of this project—and it will definitely be completed sooner or later—helps us understand that the existentially most challenging consequence of the electronic age has been the elimination of the dimension of space from multiple levels of our experience and our behavior. If we understand that the process of electronic socialization, while of course not synonymous with globalization, is its most powerful source of energy, we can discover a fascinating paradox. Supported by electronics, globalization has both expanded and strengthened our control over the space of the planet (to which we have recently returned to limit ourselves) up to a perhaps insuperable degree; at the same time, it has almost completely excluded space from our existence.

And we are not only talking about the speed with which information can travel today and about the unheard of quantities in which it is available and circulates —as if space did not matter anymore. Personally, I cannot forget that balmy Friday evening at Rio de Janeiro, when I met with some friends at a beautiful restaurant at Botafogo Beach, under Sugar Loaf, where I saw, close to us, a table with four gorgeous young people, obviously two couples, where all four managed to be on their cell phones with other people at some point. It does not really matter whether they were talking to other friends in Rio or to people who were somewhere else (perhaps far away in New Zealand); the point was that, despite the unbeatably beautiful environment in which they found themselves, the young people's attention was separated, in each of the four cases, from the place where their bodies were. Or, more dramatically: the position of their bodies had become completely irrelevant for the activities of their minds. From the perspective of this scene, which is so typical of our everyday, it becomes clear that the origins of globalization go back much further than to the early nineteenth century. If the capacity to separate our minds from our bodies has been a condition (and, more recently, also a consequence) of globalization, then globalization becomes coextensive with the process of modernization, as it depends on and begins with the Cartesian formula of human self-reference: "I think, therefore I am" or, more precisely for our own time, "I produce, circulate, and receive information, therefore I am." Both formulas presuppose the exclusion of the human body (and of space as the dimension of its articulation) from the understanding and definition of what it is to be human.[4]

This means that, if globalization has increased, for most of us, the likelihood of taking a picture, with our digital cameras, of the Taj Mahal, the Sidney Opera House, or the baroque churches of Ouro Preto, it has also diminished the intensity with which the things of the world are present to us, in the sense of being tangible. While it would be difficult to argue that a relationship of "presence" and "tangibility" is a truly "better" relationship to the material world that surrounds us than a relationship based on experience and information, it is interesting to see that many tourists today do not really know how to react in the real presence of those monuments that, to see live, they have often invested serious amounts of money. So they end up taking hundreds of digital photographs that are most likely inferior in their quality to those photographs they had already seen at home on respective Web sites—and this is only one of many reasons why they will probably never have a retrospective look at all the photos they shot. Once again, I will refrain from trying to argue that this—largely "digital"—relationship to the material world is existentially inferior to a relationship based on presence. By any means, however, it seems to omit—rather than to actively exclude—some seldom-mentioned dimensions of individual life that, in reaction to this omission, seem to make themselves perceived.

5

Before we try to see which largely overlooked layers of our existence may become visible under the pressures of globalization, we should try to identify some further phenomena that affect our individual lives—for while they may all be somehow related to it, they are far from all being identical with the bracketing of space and presence. One often observed aspect is the emergence and steady growth of a specific space—a "network of channels" would be a good metaphor—that is immune to all local specifications and flavors. It is, for example, the space of large airports, which displays the logos and the design of the same few international airlines, and the cafés and duty-free shops with the brands we find everywhere else (both in their original version and, especially in former "Third World" countries, on the aggressively expanding market of "designer knockoffs": Starbucks and Mövenpick, Montblanc, Chanel, Armani, Dolce Gabbana, and Prada (has anyone ever mentioned that Italian brands— and Italian food in general—have been much more dominant and successful in this particular market than the United States, whose unfortunate McDonald Golden Arches—not to speak of the unspeakable Ronald McDonald himself—are much more frequently spoken about and much more frequently blamed?). Now, what that excellent film about being Lost in Translation tried to illustrate is the ongoing expansion and perfection of this emblematic channel of globalization, to the point of being inescapable. For it now leads you from the airport to your hotel downtown Tokyo or downtown Moscow, and from there of course—preferably in an air-conditioned bus—to the main historical sites, monuments, and museums of those cities, before it takes you back to the airport.

Therefore, it has become difficult to find any situations that deserve to be called situations of "lived experience" (which is the English translation of the German concept *Erleben*), in the sense of being situations for which we do not have ready-made concepts, a well-laid approach, and, in the worst case, even tickets and a tourist guide. This development explains the no longer so new—and inevitably paradoxical—tendency within the tourist industry today to provide their clients with "adventure vacations" (or, in the German speaking countries, with *Erlebnis-Urlauben*). Meanwhile, those sectors of big cities and exotic countries that might provide adventures and *Erlebnisse* have become too dangerous and too secluded to visit. Brazilian *favelas*, for example, have probably never been these romantic places full of samba and passionate love by which *Orfeo Negro*, a beautiful Italo-French and Brazilian coproduction from the 1950s, depicted them—but today no curious tourist could survive there even one single night, for all his or her potentially very good intentions.

English has become the *koiné*, the common language, of our globalized world (with Castilian Spanish being a remote second)—despite all the aggressive and politically correct efforts to avoid such a development. Without any doubt, this had much more to do with certain internal properties of the English language (properties that it largely shares with Castilian) than with the role of the United States as a former hegemonic power—and I am not emphasizing this point to "defend" the United States but because I want to illustrate how globalization as a process resembles evolution rather than a planned political action or operation. What gave the status of a *koiné* to the English language is the fact that, due to a comparatively low complexity on the levels of morphology, syntax, and pronunciation, learners can quickly reach an elementary competence that enables them to participate in basic forms of communication. The well-known flip side of this advantage lies in the fact that, individually, many speakers never reach a level beyond "pidgin" practice—which fact, for large parts of their everyday communicative practice, reduces the range of expression to an unacceptable minimum. In addition, and different from those languages whose structures and conventions are held stable through institutions with an authoritative status, such as the French language and the Académie Française (the Real Academia Española fulfills a similar function, but is less rigid), English appears to be extremely tolerant with pidgin users, up to the point of being receptive to certain deviations from the linguistic norm that they produce. It is therefore possible to imagine that the comparative softness of the English language as a cultural institution converges with a historical environment—ours—that is eager (or at least ready) to embrace the informal style of "governance" in its operations and interactions and that encourages us to live oscillating between different time zones. In this sense our world is different indeed from the world of the seventeenth and eighteenth centuries when French was the *koiné* and the belief in the authoritative power and dignity of "rational" solutions was unlimited (implying that there always was one and only one correct solution per problem).

Today, by contrast, brand name producers are too weary to legally pursue designer knockoffs and grammarians judge pidgin usages to be "productive." Some critical minds will say that such accumulated sloppiness reaches its dramatic extreme, an extreme with irreversible consequences for our planet, in the acceptance of air traveling (and other forms of locomotion based on combustion) as a basic practice and precondition of globalization and thus as a condition for our increasing independence from physical space—despite their truly devastating ecological consequences. A possible response to such criticism could be that our growing awareness of such ecological "footprints" shows that we have at least begun to react to the excesses of globalization.

6

Let me insist: the increasing independence of information from physical space and the impression that human existence at large may soon reach a similar state seem to have activated a new awareness of some basic needs of humankind. Here lies the potential of a negative anthropology opened by globalization. But I also want to mention that the current desire to recuperate the dimensions of body and space can well be explained through a different argument, an argument that does not refer to globalization. From a philosophical standpoint and from a standpoint of epistemological history, it makes sense to say that the Cartesian—i.e., bodiless—idea of being human used to be associated with a specific dimension of the present in the historicist construction of time, that is, with the present being "merely transitional" as it had being taken for granted within historicism. Adapting experience from the past to the conditions of present and future, the subject used to choose, in the short present, among the many opportunities that the future seemed to offer. This, to choose among multiple possibilities of the future, based on experience from the past, is what we used to call an action.

Today we increasingly feel that our present has broadened, as it is now surrounded by a future we can no longer see, access, or choose and a past that we are not able to leave behind. If, however, the Cartesian subject was dependent on the (historicist) present as a present of mere transition, then the new, ever broadening present can no longer be the present of the Cartesian subject. This view seems to explain our renewed concern with the physical aspects of human existence and with space as the dimension in which they emerge against the grain of the Cartesian tradition—and it would not necessarily contradict a view of the same effects of bodilessness as a consequence of globalization, i.e., the approach that we have been pursuing so far. For one could claim, among others things, that the new, posthistoricist construction of time too is a reaction to phenomena and effects of globalization.

Without any doubt, the most visible—and indeed ubiquitous—symptom of the desire and need to recuperate the bodily dimension of human existence is the institution of sports, as they have developed, in a both massive and complex way, since the beginning of the nineteenth century. Never before had they penetrated to all social groups and enclaves; never did they have the powerful economic articulation and, most important, the central existential importance that they have for us today.[5] Sport in Ancient Greece was the privilege of a small elite—whereas, between the fifth century BC and the nineteenth century, its presence has been astonishingly discontinuous. From the decades following 1800, by contrast, it became coupled, for the first time, as a noble activity that would ultimately strengthen the mind, to the educational systems in all Western societies, while team sports with professional athletes, from the last quarter of the same century on, began to attract larger crowds than ever before. If a tension between ("noble") amateur sports and ("mercenary") professional sports had developed into a stable structure during the first half of the twentieth century, the discovery of athletic activity as a device of proactive health care since the 1950s has now produced a symbiosis between, on the one side, top athletes in all events, who can earn large amounts of money based on media coverage and advertising (mainly for athletic apparel and clothes), and, on the other hand, a collective participatory body that probably counts in the billions today, a body of people who both practice sports and make watching sports a primary leisure activity. And, with teams and athletes who emphasize their national, regional, and local affiliations, sports not only provide an impression of recovering the physical side of human existence, they also bind our imagination and experienced back to specific places—and they often do so, paradoxically, through global broadcasting.

Beside sports and beside certain auto-aggressive practices like piercing, tattooing, and self-cutting that seem to be driven by a vague desire for "grounding" oneself in the material world, gender is a further dimension in which globalized culture has begun to reclaim layers of physical existence, thus compensating for previous losses. The process goes along with a progressive (although not always ideally successful) neutralization of gender in the professional sphere, based on basic values and rights of equality. For if women, during the past hundred years, have been allowed for the first time to excel as academics, politicians, engineers, or soccer players, and if the social pressure for men to be high achieving and dominant has diminished, these changes have been accompanied by a new eagerness to experience the "essence" and essential consequences of gender as a physical difference. The assumption that women and men feel, experience, and perhaps even think in very different ways has become part of our everyday as a frequent conversation topic and as a premise of many interactions. And we are now taking the next step by conceiving of gender as a nonbinary distinction.

The one reaction to globalization and globalization effects that has long been understood as such is the political tendency toward regionalization. Nowhere is it easier to grasp and to study than in the European Union and, within the European Union, in Spain. This development appears all the more impressive and all the more astonishing against the backdrop of the undeniable political and economic success that the European Union once enjoyed. Of course, each "region" within Spain that has emphasized its cultural identity and claimed rights of political independence, and each European nation-state, like the United Kingdom, Denmark, or France in recent years, that has tried to slow down the process of European integration has valid historical, social, and legal reasons. But along with the fact that regional customs, regional styles, regional gastronomy— indeed, anything regional—have become so important, even in those countries inside and outside Europe whose populations seem to be content with their current national constitution and identity, like Germany or France, the new appetite for the regional gives evidence to an existential need. It is the need for belonging to a space that is not too large to be filled with personal experience or at least with personal imagination. Part of such a desire for the specific is a new fascination with national languages and their dialects as devices of world appropriation that have been shaped through their locales and histories. By comparison, the circuits of global traffic where we so easily get "lost in translation," and even the concepts and emblems that stand for the European Union or other political federations, are too abstract to produce such feelings of belonging.

The interference of different time zones as an experience and especially the juxtaposition of different historical times in our broadening present have produced a similar need for what I would like to call temporal scale. If it has become increasingly difficult for us to "leave behind" any past, partly because of our new powerful technologies of recording and memory preservation, partly because of the aforementioned transformation in our social construction of time, we have greater difficulties today than in the past of saying what would be the architecture, the literary style, or the music "of our time." While there may be no easy remedy for this situation of historical entropy, many of us find relief in the production of historically coherent environments. There is, for example, a regional airline in Brazil whose cabins and uniforms try to copy, as closely as possible, the Pan Am style of the 1950s. The same is true for many baseball stadiums built in the United States during the past twenty years, as they try to conjure up the atmosphere of athletic events in the early twentieth century.

But these phenomena of compensation seem to be quite marginal in relation to the final two tendencies that I want to describe. Together with the vanishing of our dreams about the conquest of space, the process of globalization has triggered a powerful and very visible movement to reclaim the planet Earth as the habitat of humankind. For we have realized, in the first place, that there may be no other habitable space for us in the universe and, in the second place, that our culture and our technologies may jeopardize those properties of the home planet on which our survival depends. This movement may be the one dimension where a desire to compensate for effects of globalization converge with globalization itself: ecological awareness as the will to minimize certain globalization effects can profit from the efficiency of global communication and its technologies in order to promote attitudes of worldwide solidarity.

The final tendency that I want to talk about is equally powerful but, at least until now, much less visible. I am referring to the central intuition of a book (*Du musst dein Leben ändern*) that the German philosopher Peter Sloterdijk published in 2009.[6] Without much speculation about possible historical or social reasons that may have produced this phenomenon, Sloterdijk observes that, during the past hundred years and now increasingly, individuals in Western cultures have been obsessed with "exercise" (the German word is *üben*), that is, with the individual acquisition of skills and with efforts of individual self-transformation, on more and more competitive levels without any ultimate limits. Already, at first glance, we can discover an interesting parallel—or convergence—with one of the three elementary conditions of human life today that we identified at the beginning of this essay. Instead of delegating human labor to "robots," i.e., to machines with the status of servants or even slaves, as centuries of the utopian imagination had propagated, we have entered a dynamic of transforming ourselves, individually and collectively, in our prosthetic fusion with computers. "Self-reflexivity and self-transformation" seems to be the combined formula of our present rather than dominance and delegation. This is where Sloterdijk's diagnosis meets our own reflections. In addition, I would like to complete Sloterdijk's description with the historical thesis that self-reflexive and self-transforming "exercise" may respond to and compensate for a situation, i.e., the world of globalization, in which institutional contours are blurred and obligatory patterns of interaction are hard to identify. In confrontation with ourselves, we establish an existential framework that our cultural environment refuses to provide. If, for example, the organizational structure of most Silicon Valley companies is horizontal, in the sense of nonhierarchical, and if the different employees of a firm hardly ever work together in a shared space, then their success can only depend on an outstanding degree of self-motivation and self-guided transformation. Self-reference replaces institutional structures. To phrase the same thought in a dystopian tonality: the brave new world of our globalized present condemns us to be our own Big Brothers. Or, in alternative milder words: in the neoliberal world of globalization we are free to constantly reinvent ourselves.

7

Before trying to make a judgment—or a more synthetic statement—about the anthropological view opened by those multiple reactions to the process of globalization, I would like to briefly mention two phenomena that I find emblematic—in complementary ways—for two basic structural aspects in which information is becoming detached from specific physical places. The first of them is a new type of worldwide celebrity and stardom that has no particular ground or reason—Paris Hilton is the name that unavoidably comes to mind (but also the names of David and Victoria Beckham, whose respective achievements in soccer and in popular music have at no moment matched the massive presence of their faces in multiple media and omnipresent commercials). While it is, of course, not the function of these media protagonists to embody or to represent anything at all (rather, their lives are characterized by the blatant absence of a function or of any other assignment), they may be part of a restless intransitive movement typical of the condition in which we become detached from space. In this view, Paris Hilton's and the Beckhams' historical predecessors were those privileged "cosmopolitans" and those hardworking "playboys" who accompanied the emergence of the railroad network and of the network of airlines in the nineteenth and in the twentieth centuries. The second phenomenon emblematic of the detachment of information from space is incomparably more incisive and dangerous. I am referring to the so-called derivative monetary instruments that have been identified as the central reason for the dramatic financial crisis that hit the world in 2008. "Derivatives" are instruments that are supposed to produce revenue independently of any object or of any business "of reference" that they would stand for or be in touch with. It is the type of detachment that creates the risk of economic implosion in situations where a collective need arises to cash them in.[7]

Here, too, I will not engage in an apocalyptic critique of globalization as the "reason" for that very recent finance disaster of global dimensions, if it were only in order to avoid any ungrounded optimism regarding the possibility of controlling such processes. Globalization and its consequences may well be part of a specific stage in the evolution of humankind where culture and technology have replaced biology as the source of energy that drives all change. But, while we may not be able to change them, we have seen how the effects of globalization provoke certain reactions—reactions of inertia sometimes—and with them the impression that the dynamics of globalization are no longer in synchrony with very basic human needs and human limits. *We want to recuperate the human body as a core dimension of individual existence; we want to claim specific places, specific regions, and the planet Earth as spheres of "home" to which we belong; we enjoy being wrapped into (artificially produced, but) coherent historical environments; we are longing for languages that open up and are shaped by the specific spaces that we call ours; and we want to give our existence orientation and goals through self-reflexive activities of "exercising."*

This list of converging conditions and needs that, in the most literal sense of the word, give us a place and bind us to the earth, is mindful of the "fourfold" (*das Geviert*) as a central motif in the final stage of Martin Heidegger's philosophy.[8] The four conditions that frame our individual existence according to Heidegger (earth, sky, godhead, mortals—*mortals* both in the sense of our fellow humans and that of our own mortality) look more symmetrical and also more mythological than the "anthropology" we have extracted from our own reflections on globalization and its effects. But both lists are very similar, not to say synonymous, inasmuch as they describe, in Heidegger's words, "dwelling" as "the manner in which mortals are on the earth" and as they include the intuition that "the basic character of dwelling is to spare, to preserve." Even closer to the conclusions we have arrived at is the work of the Italianist and philosopher Robert Harrison, who, in three different books that make for one complex argument, has concentrated on forests, burial places, and gardens in order to elaborate what I would like to call a new ecological Existentialism.[9]

The preface to Hannah Arendt's magnificent book, *The Human Condition*, from 1958, resonates with the powerful reactions that the launching of

Sputnik, the first artificial satellite, caused just one year earlier.[10] Arendt took issue with the then often-expressed view that Sputnik had been "the first step toward escape from men's imprisonment to the earth." She objected because she believed the cosmological identity of human existence to depend on the fact that the very condition of "culture" and its layers of "labor," "work," and "action" were all grounded in life—and "life" meant for her that they were all sustained by our biological connection to the Earth. This participation of human existence in two different but inseparable dimensions, which Arendt called "artificial" (culture) and "natural" (life), explains why human birth and death, why "natality" and "mortality" (in her own terminology), must be different from the birth and death of all other living beings. Should we ever become severed definitively from the Earth, we will lose that identity and with it the ability to labor, to work, and to act.

Recent developments have confirmed the core of Arendt's anticipation and concern. With the one difference, of course, that it was not space traveling that jeopardized the existential condition of dwelling—but electronic communication, the most important basis and the most important consequence of globalization.

III. STAGNATION

Temporal, Intellectual, Heavenly

On the way to the dinner being held for conference participants at a Georgian restaurant near the Kremlin, two colleagues from Moscow who, in the final years of the Soviet Union, had managed to find another life at Oxford and in New York, gave the American a brief cultural tour. Here was Mayakovsky's residence at the beginning of the October Revolution, there the dwelling of the young Pasternak. In front of the department store with a clock telling the time across the globe, they had stood as young boys; with the feverish patriotism of children, they heard how the first Sputnik had started its course around the planet. This event, Andreij affirms, marked the highpoint of the seven-odd decades granted to the communist republic to realize its utopias. When, asks the American, did Soviet citizens cease to believe that Marxist-Leninist promises would be fulfilled and turn to despair and defeatism?

Remarkably, the two hosts who are back at home from vacation, agree completely: it was only in the final Brezhnev years that, almost overnight—but then very rapidly—a pessimistic mood became widespread or, maybe, it was after the last party secretary to be more or less respected by Soviet society had died—during a period that, already then, was called the time of stagnation. The answer astounds the foreigner, who promptly remarks his own incomprehension. Isn't

he sure that communism had already become intolerable to the people it promised to set free when the so-called Stalinist show trials occurred in the 1930s?
Doesn't he recall the fear that seized Western adults—in 1956, when the upris-
ing in Hungary was quashed, or in 1957, when Sputnik was launched—that the
triumphant Soviet Union would dominate the globe? Hadn't he himself—and
in a rather partisan manner—celebrated the end of the Vietnam War as the
triumph of socialist solidarity over his own land?

1

Another, much less dramatic stagnation has also befallen the tiny world of
his professional existence, the world of the humanities. When he attended
school—and still in the late 1960s, when he began university studies—works of
philosophy and literature were to be examined "for their own sake." "Immanent-
ly," one said at the time—more in a "congenial" spirit than in terms of a method.

Then, all at once—as students in Berkeley, Paris, and Berlin started to take
their somewhat stubborn displeasure at the tired world of their parents for
revolutionary energy—"paradigms" conquered the most remote corners of the
university establishment: structuralism, with its seemingly mathematical precision; Marxism, which augured truth and transformation; formalism, which had
a Russian origin that people mistook for a Soviet pedigree; and reception theory, with its legitimately social-democratic promise. Before long, the philosophy
of science initiated by Thomas S. Kuhn explained why such changes deserved
to be called "paradigm shifts." Illusions of various colorations about "social rel-
evancy" combined with a deadly earnest belief in "scientificity."

When apprehensions arose that the world might not, after all, dance to a
score composed by humanists, there appeared, as if on cue, much gentler theories, which were less fixated on scientificity and pointed in the opposite direction. For the most part, they came from France and were therefore, under a
grammatically singular rubric that imposed excessive uniformity, called French
theory. Michel Foucault both startled and calmed his readers with the message that power (and many other things, too) consisted of nothing but "dis-
cursive" configurations. The deconstruction of Jacques Derrida (and Paul de
Man) declared a taboo on both pronounced conceptual distinctions and refined
arguments; this encouraged its adherents to comport themselves like the initi-
ates of a new society of freemasons, even though it was not necessarily clear
why standing distinctions were to be avoided. Then came the new historicism,

which owed only trace elements to France, with its relaxed assurances that historiography was just another literary genre.

Before ideologically incensed scholars could formulate the question, filled with reproach, of whether Foucault, Derrida, and the new historicism had betrayed the theories and values of the classical left, a scientifically and politically programmatic atmosphere clouded the skies again: even if it was, perhaps, a humanistic mishmash of everything under the sun, cultural studies promised empirical precision and engagement in the struggle for the recognition of all kinds of identities. Academically, at any rate, there was no room for levity. In Germany cultural studies combined with a conviction of a fundamentalist stripe that the future would lie in concentrating on "media" from the perspective of engineers as critical users.

The veritable profusion of paradigms occurred in the 1980s. Since then the movement back and forth between "hard" and "soft" theories has stagnated and the serial production of paradigms has dried up. In the humanities today, many books worthy of notice—perhaps greater in number than ever before—are published. Young university colleagues seem more and more educated, students appear more industrious than ever before, and research projects are duly "assigned" to them. Small towns like Marbach am Neckar preserve the archives of authors belonging to the past and the future (the future past) alike. Everything follows its abnormally normal course, even though, today, nobody knows where the cutting edge makes its mark. The deluge of paradigms raining down in rhythmical chain reactions that once roused the older generation now rests, at home and in libraries, on the shelves of "theory," where books that stand as far from each other as they do from life itself are grouped together.

2

It seems like a grotesque coincidence that the humanities and state socialism lapsed into pools of stagnation at the same time. However, one can picture a common source of energy that fed them for decades and has now run dry. This source may have been "historical consciousness." This "social construction of time"—this chronotope—emerged in the early nineteenth century and, as the institutional precondition for human behavior and actions, held such enormous consequences that it was simply confused with "time" and "history" until philosophically ambitious historians—especially Michel Foucault and Reinhart Koselleck—began to historicize it too.

If one grants, as I mentioned in the introduction, that, around 1800 (or, to adopt a somewhat more flexible periodization, in the years between 1780 and 1830, which Koselleck dubbed the saddle period), intellectual and scholarly life took on the habit of practicing self-observation while observing the world,[1] one can understand how the impression arose that, for every object of the world—and in keeping with the perspectives of multiple observers—there must exist a potential infinity of "representations" or "interpretations." Such perspectivism transformed into an epistemological *horror vacui*, that is, into a fear, when faced with the irrepressible multiplicity of representations and interpretations, that there was perhaps nothing in the world wholly self-identical and stable.

A solution to this problem—or, more precisely, a response that had a sufficiently powerful effect to make the problem fall into oblivion—involved exchanging the principle of apprehending the world as if in a mirror (a scheme in which there exists one—and only one—representation/interpretation per object) for narrative ways to understand it. This occurred in the philosophy of history (including—even especially—its popular varieties) and evolutionary schemes à la Darwin. Such realignment offers a solution to the problem of perspectivism because narrative discourses make it possible to synthesize multiple representations as identical objects by arranging them in sequence and making them appear, as moments of transformation, to be the inevitable effects of time. Thus, for example, to answer the question "What is Prussia?" it became necessary to tell the history of Prussia. It followed the same logic that evolutionary speculation was soon thought to provide the best answers to questions concerning the essence of mankind.

This experience of the world and the things that constitute it as movement, as a history within histories—as well as the desire to experience the world in this way—provided the source of energy that, in the early nineteenth century, charged the "theoretical curiosity" already awakened in the Renaissance with unprecedented political, economic, and cultural dynamism, yielding an intoxicating drive for innovation. Foucault called it the *historisation des êtres*. Out of the confluence there arose, before long, a new image of the past—the picture of history that we call historicism. At its center stood a conception of self-referentiality that had become more complex—of "man" as an intellectual being and a principle of movement. Now, as Koselleck pointedly remarked, humanity was seen in time, constantly leaving behind pasts as "spheres of experience" and striding forward into ever new futures shaped by open "horizons of possibilities." Between these futures and those pasts, the present manifested itself as a "mere moment of transition"; experienced in this way, it offered the Cartesian subject, concentrated solely on functions of consciousness, its historical habitat.

The role of this subject was to align experiences from the past with conditions of the present and the future and to select, from the possibilities the future afforded, projects for a transformed world that were always new. Such is the operation of *Handeln* described by the first sociologists in the nineteenth century—which some philosophers consider the core of human existence to this very day.

At their historical high points, both socialism and capitalism shared historical consciousness as the chronotope of progress and, for this reason, as a common foundation and energy reserve for motivation. Today, to be sure, there is reason to believe that the chronotope of progress already imploded decades ago, even if our discourses, for purposes of communication and self-understanding, still perpetuate it. In the early 1980s—that is, when a feeling of stagnation began to become widespread among Soviet citizens while, elsewhere, the humanities were sailing on the penultimate wave of euphoric innovation—Jean-François Lyotard published *La condition postmoderne* and directed the critical attention of countless Western intellectuals to the *grand récits* as "totalizing" discourses. Thereby, a foundational premise of historical consciousness after 1800—in which it found the answer to the problem of perspectivism, and behind which it had marched triumphantly through epistemology and the everyday—imploded. The assumption collapsed that for every object in the world there exists only one narrative representation. All at once, it became clear that an infinite potential of possible histories about Prussia could be activated, just as there existed an infinite array of histories about the development of Homo sapiens.

When the premise of historical consciousness fell, the historicizing view of human movement through time shifted, I believe, to the (sometimes uncomfortable) terrain of temporal stasis and simultaneity. By no means, in the early twenty-first century, does the future present itself as a horizon of open possibilities for action (*Handeln*). Instead, the future is drawing near—those familiar with the Middle Ages know temporal structures of this kind—with threatening scenarios that cannot be calculated in detail: take, for example, "global warming," nuclear catastrophe, or the potential consequences of overpopulation. Faced with the prospect of such scenarios becoming a reality, we seek to gain a delay, at best; but we hardly believe anymore that disaster can be averted once and for all. At the same time, the border between the past and the present seems to have become porous. German intellectuals, in particular, are of fond of celebrating this displacement as a turn to a nebulous "something better," which they call *Memoria-Kultur*. However, the problematic consequences of pasts flooding the present cannot be foreseen. Maybe, as Niklas Luhmann once remarked, it really isn't necessary to declare every factory chimney in eastern Westphalia a national monument to be preserved at any cost. At any rate, between those threatening futures and a present that leaves increasingly fewer traces, there has arisen— out of the one "barely perceptible short moment" that Baudelaire described in *Peintre de la vie moderne*—an ever expanding presence of simultaneities.[2] In this present it is impossible to forget anything, yet at the same time—because we are inclined to turn our backs on the future for reasons that, although reasonable, are not necessarily good—we no longer know in what direction we should progress.

This expanding present, where experiences accumulate until they become a burden, no longer offers a dwelling to the Cartesian subject, that is, to the self-reference of modern tradition. Perhaps this explains why, since the end of the twentieth century, new conceptions of self-reference (such as the "reappropriation of the body" or the "rational reenchantment of the world") have been discussed with growing intensity.[3] The new present is, above all, a present whose relationship to the future turns belief in progress and the ambitious projects it entails into a stagnant mood of something deeper than depression. It is possible to oppose, to the impression that this new chronotope is now in place, "objective" statistics of continuity and even renewal, but numbers and empirical values are not the real issue. Rather, it is a matter of time as a "form of experience," as Edmund Husserl defined it: a social construction of time, which determines how we turn changes we perceive in our environment into a relationship we entertain with our selves and our actions. I will not ask for the "reasons" behind this—presumed—change of chronotope, just as I haven't sought the "reasons" and epistemological conditions for the emergence of historical thinking in the early nineteenth century. The contexts in which questions of this kind assume their full significance are too complex—without an extensive discussion of details, at any rate—to permit answers that are not tautological.

3

A development that has only recently come into view might confirm the impression that the chronotope of historical consciousness collapsed after an epoch of continuous paradigm shift. On the one hand, as an academic and institutional structure, the humanities are some two hundred years old; most of the disciplines that today compose them go back to the age of romanticism. At the same time, they preserve an impulse and form of self-understanding that already existed among the philologists at the museum of Alexandria. This legacy involves saving (mainly textual) documents from material erosion and oblivion—the desire to collect works against dispersal in space, whether in the recesses of a library or in the archives of a discipline.

The obsolescence of both functions appears imminent in light of electronic communications technology, which has introduced a vision of the future where all the documents that humanity has at its disposal, whether textual or non-textual, can be produced on the screen of any laptop.[4] Should this situation occur—and only juridical instances will provide a serious obstacle—the innovative energy of the humanities will hardly be curtailed, even if they lose one of the central tasks that have sustained them until now (as well as the potential for legitimation it affords). Yet electronic technology's power to collect and preserve will intensify a problem that was already announced when the historicizing paradigm imploded. This problem involves the difficulty of selecting objects for sustained attention on the basis of prognostications about the future under increased conditions of complexity. From the time of ancient oratory until recently, *copia*—the possession of an extensive vocabulary—was a chief virtue. Today the computer has made knowledge accessible at levels of previously unimaginable scope and density—at the same time, however, its use raises a question: What is this knowledge good for?

4

A new kind of intellectual has emerged. Thanks to the skilled mastery of electronic technologies—but also through a patient reading of the classics—s/he thinks s/he knows where the answer to every question can be found. S/he is a kinsman of the scholar that General Stumm von Bordwehr sought in vain at the "world-famous court library" of Vienna in Musil's *Man Without Qualities*. Responding to the general's request for a "summary of all great thoughts of humanity," the court librarian offered disheartening words. "*Herr General*, you would like to know how I know every book? I can only tell you it's because of this: I don't read any of them!"

Like Musil's librarian, our computers know every book. They surpass him, however, because they have "read" all the books, "remembered" their contents, and stand at the disposal of competent users who know the right questions to ask. This fact explains why, at humanities colloquia, younger participants impress their predecessors with the depth of their knowledge of detailed issues and often produce real textual discoveries. For all that, however, the will to synthesize materials, the courage to make an argument that changes critical perspectives, and even the pleasure to be found in speculation have clearly receded.

Among scholars, synthesis, theses, and learned conjecture have fallen into disrepute, even when it is clear that they are not binding or empirically demonstrable. Perhaps the excesses of the most significant intellectual authorities of the present are merely tolerated by their successors—nothing more. When those who will soon retire were beginning their careers—at the great hour of structuralism, linguistics, and Noam Chomsky—it was common to hear (as if a threat were being issued) that soon a "grammar" would be written for a given cultural phenomenon. Such grammars were intended to occupy a point where an intuitive grasp of essences merged with innovation. Nothing could be further from the minds of young scholars today than this kind of intellectual ambition—a fact that isn't necessarily a symptom of academic decadence.

5

The rise of the chronotope of the broad present, I have suggested, led to the loss of the historically specific frame of development for the classical Cartesian subject. Symptoms confirming this thesis were found through the now commonplace philosophical and pseudo-philosophical efforts to reinstall, in the superannuated conception of the subject, components of existence such as the body, space, presence, and the senses. The dimension of *Handeln*—that is, the possibility of permanently transforming (and thereby renewing) the world— would be much less important for a subject whose self-reference included the body as it did before modernity, for such subjectivity was inhibited (or at least severely restricted) in its ability to think about the future in terms of scenarios to be changed through conscious action—a set of presuppositions to which we are accustomed today that we still make without a second thought.

Instead, I would further speculate, it would be necessary to foreground a tendency that strikes us as archaic: to find in the world—as it occurs to us spatially and temporally in recurring cycles of habit and custom—the "right" places for the human body and mind, that is, to inscribe one's being into the material world physically and spiritually.[5] Doing so would be a form of the being-in-the-world that Heidegger analyzes in *Being and Time*. Institutions that enable self-inscription of this kind are called rituals. The definition implies a question: has a functional change in culture, which has transformed it into the sphere of ritual, led to the new status of knowledge and the modes in which it is now produced? A functional change of this kind would place culture in strong opposition to the classical assertion that art—precisely because of its "autonomy" and distance from the everyday world—acts as a permanent agent of irritation, provocation, and change in society.

6

Recently—in the city of General Stumm von Bordwehr, at that—the American recently had a conversation with a philosopher, and he was reminded that culture is a sphere of ritual. They had met for dinner on the terrace of a restaurant in the Viennese "museum district." The museum district lies not far, as one heads out from the city center, from the Hofburg. Remarkably, it can compete with the Hofburg in size and stands surrounded by museums (of course), theaters, concert halls, institutions for promoting artistic endeavors, as well as buildings that house their copies in academic form.

There, on a proverbially warm early summer evening, among the ambitious (and, in some cases, truly beautiful) buildings, there strolled hundreds—or perhaps even thousands—of young people as well as retired couples striving for youth and, naturally, people of prime working age seeking diversion. They sat on stone benches, immersed in friendly conversations that sometimes seemed to take a passionate turn, waited in line for tickets, or simply took pleasure in the sandwich or bag of chips they had brought along. On this day, which was no more special than any other, the financially robust Austrian government had a right to quote, with self-satisfaction, the observation made in Goethe's *Faust*. Here, in the museum district, lay its "people's true heaven," for great and small alike could display and experience their humanity. ("Here is the people's paradise, / And great and small shout joyously: / Here I am human, may enjoy humanity.")

The Viennese philosopher alone seemed unsatisfied—grumpy, even. An extended stay in New York not too long ago, he reported, had been a great disappointment. He had encountered nothing of cultural value there: the opera was conventional, the dramas staged in a commercial fashion, and the performance of the orchestra sloppy. He had returned with a sense of certainty, which was altogether edifying for his national pride, that Vienna was the cultural capital of the world. In the middle of the museum district, sitting before his goulash, the American didn't feel like offering a patriotic rebuttal or agreeing in wholehearted self-criticism. "Cultural capital of the world" was aiming a little high, he commented sympathetically, but "world capital of event culture" might be a more fitting honorific for contemporary Vienna.

Only when he heard himself speak did it occur to him how much the museum district was a site of ecstatic event culture—whereby the phrase *ecstatic event culture* sounds like a bit of an oxymoron, inasmuch the "events" of the present tend to avoid the sudden overwhelming rush that defines ecstasy. At any rate, the central form of event culture, he thought, in a further association, is, of course, the curator. Finally, he understood why the verb *curate* had enjoyed such a rapid ascent in the cultural sections of German-language newspapers for the past few years. After all, the curator is an embodiment—quite possibly the very incarnation—of the new intellectual: a producer of culture who knows, first and foremost, where to find what kind of knowledge—and, in his specific profession, where to find what cultural objects. Additionally, he has the ability to stage this knowledge and these objects in space, so that parties who visit the exhibitions he curates can find their place in culture in a wholly literal sense: they move, with attention and sometimes even reverence, through the array of things displayed. The curator isn't concerned with innovation—dynamism like that tends to make him nervous—but with reviving the experiential qualities stored in objects acquired over the centuries.

The programs of the theaters and opera houses in Vienna and other cultural capitals of the West have long since assumed this function. The number of new dramas, operas, and compositions that are staged is kept to a minimum—just enough to refute the potential criticism that productive contemporary artists are being denied the support they deserve according to the social-democratic conception of justice. At the center of all exalted event cultures stand more and more perfect productions of the classics. Here—besides formal accomplishment that deserves true admiration—provocative and, to be sure, iconoclastic ideas are not at all important (as was the case in the *Regietheater* of the recent past); instead, it is a matter of presenting refined nuances in permanent variation. The last "production" of *Rosenkavalier* can only be truly appreciated by someone who has had enough time to attend all the stagings that preceded it. Nuances within a world in which the same returns—such is the formula of the serial events comprising our culture.

7

The formulaic return of nuance also loosens the received hierarchies of quality and cultural *niveau*. The celestial tones of compositions by Johann Strauss, the king of the waltz, and the champagne world of operetta await rediscovery alongside lesser-known operas by Richard Strauss. As if to provide an allegory for this kind of democratic leveling, the area between the Hofburg and the museum district was reserved for spectators in the 2008 World Cup. Whoever, in the manner of Adorno or even out of genuine political conviction, voiced criticism of this kind of arrangement looked hopelessly out-of-date or—and this is much worse in the world of the European Union—shamelessly elitist. This is the case because art has never had as many upright admirers as it does in the twenty-first century—parties who cannot be numbered in the ranks of the *Bildungsbürgertum* or the "cultural aristocracy."

Today, *Bildung* occurs as a lifelong process of self-formation. It is never too late to "get on board," since its program values propaedeutic discourses and exercises much more than did the old model, when education was osmotically absorbed, so to speak, with traditional "good manners." The matter calls to mind the form of temporality that Helmut Schmidt, the erstwhile chancellor, joked about when he suggested that the end of education would soon coincide with retirement; at the same time, it recalls the mode of temporal existence suffused with the ethos of nonbinding relationships one finds in the notion of "partners for different stages of life." Yet whatever spiteful turn taken by commentaries in which we, the intellectuals of yesterday, engage the new, dominant reality, that is, the artistic formation of event culture, easily surpasses even the most audacious dreams of the German idealists of the early nineteenth century—a fact that renders idle many, if not all, our prejudices and objections.

Perhaps the process of permanent artistic formation—training for event culture—is even in the process of negating the "autonomy of art" that philosophical idealists once formulated. Ironically, this also would mean the fulfillment of a central utopia animating the historical avant-garde. I would not maintain that the "autonomy of art," which is alternately viewed as sublime and lamented as a limitation, has vanished into the dialectic because, now, local and multinational "sponsors" are thoroughly concerned—if not compelled by the demands of image—to make themselves popular by promoting culture. To take offense at this phenomenon—indeed, merely remarking anything special about it— would sound like cultural criticism of the most outmoded variety.

My observation that the *Aufhebung* of aesthetic autonomy has perhaps occurred refers to the fact that the discontinuity between the manifold modes of aesthetic experience and the everyday of economy and politics has possibly disappeared. In earlier times art and aesthetic experience were united in a world outside the everyday, where they offered an alternative—sometimes a heavenly one—to the prose of life. In the vehicle-free centers of new cities, museums and concert halls are built by increasingly prominent architects; between them, events shoot forth into the broad present. Government buildings and central bank offices are in the process of retreating into the anonymity of the urban periphery; they are no longer evaluated in terms of function or even security, but rather—as is the case, for example, in the newly inaugurated American embassy in Berlin—in terms of the new aesthetics of city planning. This seems like a spatial expression of the rarely mentioned fact that—in Europe, at any rate—participation in culture is in the process of pushing traditional forms of work away from the center of taxpayers' lives. Perhaps stagnation is not too high a price for such massive existential and social progress.

IV. "LOST IN FOCUSED INTENSITY"

Spectator Sports and Strategies of Re-Enchantment

Sometimes, reactions from practitioners become particularly inspiring moments in the lives of professional humanists. For only practitioners can confirm that our tentative conceptual constructions are on target and, at the same time, only they have an authority to justify the effort of pushing further certain thoughts that have begun to emerge in our minds as bold, and therefore often vague, intuitions. Such a decisive intellectual moment had arrived when, during a colloquium on "The Athlete's Body" organized by the Athletic Department and the Department of Comparative Literature at Stanford University in 1995, Pablo Morales, a three-time Olympic gold medalist in the butterfly swimming events and a Stanford alum, explained, as if in passing, how the addictive desire of "being lost in focused intensity" had brought him back to competitive sports after a first retirement and at an age that simply seemed to exclude any world-class performance in his sport.

Quite explicitly, Morales's complex concept referred both to the spectator's and the athlete's experience. For what had brought the impression of "getting lost in focused intensity" back to him as something he could not yet live without was the TV broadcast of a track-and-field event at the 1988 Olympics:

I will never forget watching the great sprinter Evelyn Ashford run as, in the anchor leg, she came from behind to win the gold medal for the United States. The race was shown through to its conclusion, after which a replay was run but this time with the camera focused on Ashford's face before, during, and after her sprint. Her eyes first panned the oval, then focused on the baton, then on the curve ahead. Oblivious to the crowd, oblivious even to her competition, I saw her lost in focused intensity. The effect was immediate. I had to remove myself from the room. But when I thought about my reaction in the ensuing hours, I came to realize what I had lost; that special feeling of getting lost in focused intensity.[1]

Pablo Morales's narrative helped me distinguish three different dimensions in the experience of sports. Firstly, the words *being lost* point to a peculiar isolation and distance of athletic events from the everyday world and its pursuits that is comparable to what Immanuel Kant called the disinterestedness of aesthetic experience. What, secondly, athletes and spectators "focus" upon—as something already present or something yet to come—belongs to the realm of epiphanies, that is, to the events of appearance, more precisely to events of appearance that show moving bodies as temporalized form. Finally, both the experience and the expectation of epiphanies are accompanied by—and then further enhance—halos of intensity, i.e., states of a quantitatively higher degree in the awareness of our emotions and of our bodies.

To describe the experience of sports as "getting lost in focused intensity" suggests that sports can become, both for athletes and spectators, a strategy of secular re-enchantment. For "being lost" converges with the definition of the *sacred* as a realm whose fascination relies on being set apart from everyday worlds; *epiphanies* belong to the dimension of re-enchantment precisely because Modernity's drive toward abstraction had always tended to replace them through "representations," i.e., through nonsubstantial modes of appearance; likewise, *intensity* marks a level in our reaction to the world and to ourselves that is normally bound to fade on the trajectory of disenchantment (which has become so strangely normative to us)—and that, by the same logic, thus turns into a predicate of re-enchantment. Even more so than in some other cases of secular reenchantment, it seems evident that we can refer to practicing sports and to watching sports as social *strategies*. For while it is not clear what exactly those practices may replace in contemporary culture, and while we do not associate a single purpose or a generalized function with them, there is an impression that the presence and the growing importance of sports today stand for something—and should indeed stand for something—that we have lost.

In four brief reflections I will try to retrieve some of those features from a formerly "enchanted" world that, most of the time half-consciously, we recuperate when we watch and practice sports. At first I will concentrate on the athlete's performance as an event that allows for (the equivalent of) miracles and I will then try to identify components of re-enchantment, above all effects of "epiphany," in the spectator's experience. My third section will be about the stadium as a "sacred" place, and I will conclude by describing a specific kind of "gratitude" that ties many spectators to the presence and to the memory of their favorite athletes.

1

Thanks to their complex theological content, reading only a few of Pindar's odes is enough to understand how victorious athletes were considered to be "heroes" in Greek antiquity, heroes without the distance or the irony that we normally imply today when we use this word—and how heroes were demigods. For there was no doubt that in the athletes' great moments of performance the power of gods—and indeed the gods themselves—became present, present in the athletes' flesh and present in space. Watching athletes compete gave their spectators the certainty to be close to the gods. The expectation that gods would be willing to engage in athletic competition was consistent with what the Greeks believed themselves to know about most of them: think of Hermes and Aphrodite, of Hephaestus, Poseidon, and, above all, of Zeus, and you will realize how the identities of those gods were built on different types of physical prowess. Both the Iliad and the Odyssey made it clear that, based on their physical strengths, these gods were constantly competing with each other, that *agon*, that is, fight and competition, was their central life form—and often indeed the only reason for them to become interested in humans at all.

The closeness of the gods whose actual presence the athletes' *agon* was supposed to help conjure up and to embody became the reason why all Pan-Hellenic Games, most visibly the games at Olympia and at Delphos, were organized around religious sanctuaries. For the appearance of the gods was a type of event supposed to become real in space—and it may well be from this premise that Martin Heidegger took the inspiration to describe what he calls the "unconcealment of Being" and the "event of Truth" through a spatial topology—i.e., as "sway," as "coming forth," and through his etymologizing interpretation of "objectivity" as getting closer in a horizontal movement.[2] At the same time, a culture that, as Ancient Greek culture seems to have done, counts on the gods' presence as a permanent possibility will not be prone to use words like *miracle* and to single out a specific dimension of the *miraculous*. Once again, however, Pindar's odes make it clear to us that the great Olympic victories were seen as events of divine presence, i.e., events that exceeded the limits of the humanly possible. One might even go so far as to speculate that the Greeks didn't care about keeping records, i.e., about how far a discus had been thrown or by how much a runner had distanced his opponents, because divine powers will ridicule any kind of measurement.

Obviously, and for many good reasons, it is considered a symptom of bad intellectual taste in present-day culture to find an athlete's performance "divine" or to appreciate its potentially record-breaking dimension as miraculous. For several decades now, different sports have triggered the development of scientifically based practicing methods—and in a number of countries this has lead to the emergence of an academic discipline quite capable of explaining away, rationally, what the Greeks took to be divine inspiration in athletic performance. Successful athletes today are all too well aware of how much they depend on the progress of highly specialized research, and they have also learned to draw a clear border between this necessary basis of their performance and what they consider to be remnants of personal superstition. How they personally live and remember their most inspired moments strongly converges with the tradition of thinking enchantment as divine presence. From this perspective, I find it telling that "being in the zone," a spatial metaphor, has become a conventional way among athletes today to invoke particularly inspired moments, moments that defy all rational explanations. Here is a description of how it feels to be in the zone written by J. R. Lemon, one of the better running backs in the history of Stanford football: "When a player has entered the zone, a state of hypersensitivity and tension has taken place. This explains the apparent ease during my run toward the end zone. It is not that I am not working as hard as the other players on the field. It is just that in this state of hypersensitivity, things are moving so much slower than they are for the rest of the players on the field. My senses are much more aware of what is going on around me and thatenables all of the triggers inside of me to react a little faster than the other players, making me appear more fluent." Obviously J. R. Lemon avoids religious language in these sentences, although he certainly does not imply that being in the zone is a state completely under the control of his intentions. A player must be physically and mentally well prepared to be open for it—but that will not be enough. What more is required for a player to be in the zone will depend, as we would say today, on whether he is "on," whether a specific game is "his" or not—it will depend on what the Greeks would have called divine inspiration.

2

If for an athlete being in the zone is a state whose arrival he is expecting "in focused intensity," the spectators' focus, especially in team sports, is on the emergence of beautiful plays. Beautiful plays are the epiphany of form. Yes, ultimately most spectators do want "their" teams to win—but if winning was all, it would be enough for them, every game day, to simply check the final scores. A beautiful play, for example J. R. Lemon receiving the ball from his quarterback and finding a hole in the other team's defensive line through which he will run the ball for another first down, is an epiphany of form because it has its substance in the participating athletes' bodies; because the form it produces is unlikely and thereby an event achieved against the resistance of the other team's defense; and finally, and above all, the beautiful play is epiphany because it is a temporalized form, a form that begins to vanish in the very process of its emergence.

For each individual spectator, such a beautiful play performed by his team produces an instant of happiness. We breathe deeply and for a moment we realize how that the players' achievement and confidence become contagious and seem to carry us. This, at least, is what most spectators hope will happen to them, most precisely—and unknowingly—all those spectators who have interiorized the game's rules and its rhythms and who do not have a professional stake in analyzing what is happening on the field, as coaches or journalists do. These spectators—we might call them the common spectators—who can afford to let their emotions go, will soon feel that they are becoming part of a larger, communal (rather than collective) body. It is within this communal body that spectators who have never met before, nor will ever meet again, feel comfortable embracing each other and it is this communal body that likes to become the movement of "the wave." Seeing itself perform such a movement and listening to the noise that it can produce at certain moments of the game provides a self-awareness that adds cohesion to the spectators' body. The spectators' communal body can become the basis for the fans to feel united to the players of their own team and may, at some rare and glorious occasions, even conquer the other team and its spectators. This was the mood when, for the opening night of Stadium Australia at Sydney, New Zealand's rugby team snapped a sensational winning streak from its archrival Australia—in what the morning newspapers, even in Australia, would unanimously celebrate as "one of the greatest matches played in the history of rugby."

There seems to be a level of participation where the enjoyment and appreciation of beautiful plays exceeds the desire for victory, where communal convergence overcomes the dynamics of rivalry. The ambiguity inherent to such moments certainly appears in other types of communal bodies, particularly those shaped by religious experience. It must have been the promise to overcome individual reclusion that motivated one of the most canonical interpretations of the Christian church as "Christ's mystical body." But history shows us how, in certain moments, the "bodies" of different denominations took shape against each other, leading to devastating religious wars, whereas, at other moments, religious communities have enthusiastically opened up for ecumenical fusion and happiness. If today the divisions separating the different interpretations and forms of Islam seem to be more irreconcilable than ever, ours is a moment prone to cocelebration within Christianity. And it may not be random that stadiums built for team sports events are used as sites for contemporary religious mass events. As long as religious communities continue to exist, it is banal—and simply inadequate—to say that sports have become "the religion of the twenty-first century." But it is obvious how sports and a renewed enthusiasm for religious experience are converging today as ways of re-enchanting the modern world.

3

Before this background it does not take great theoretical imagination to see that stadiums have the status of sacred spaces. For they gain an aura by being visibly dysfunctional, that is, by being demonstratively different from spaces and buildings that fulfill predefined functions in our everyday. From an economic point of view, no more counterintuitive gesture exists in contemporary culture than that of building new stadiums in downtown areas where the real estate is extremely expensive. For not only do sports facilities not allow for high-rise construction as it normally maximizes the efficiency of the ground acquired. Most important, stadiums are empty during most of the week and often over even longer stretches of time.

This does not only explain why empty stadiums, as sacred spaces, have an almost irresistible appeal for passionate sports fans. Above all, stadiums as sacred spaces are spaces that require and trigger layers of ritualized behavior during those comparatively short moments in which they are filled with action. Being in a stadium, both for athletes and spectators, is not primarily about inventing and showing individualized action. It is about inscribing oneself, physically, into a preexisting order that only allows for narrow spaces of variation. Every event, every country, every moment in the history of sports develop their own rituals, poses, and gestures that open up a dimension for endless individual interpretation. Think of the gradual historical transformations in the uniforms for different sports, of the changing objects of attention for halftime entertainment, or of the signs of tension or mutual respect between the players on rival teams (from archaically "sportsmanlike" correctness via openly mean antagonism to the fake friendship smile of media stars).

Through the multiplicity of such colorful developments, however, there is one structural pattern that imposes itself in any situation of spectator sports—and this form is clearly related to the nature of the stadium as sacred space. It is the contrast between moments of emptiness or inaction and moments filled with the most intense bodily activity, a contrast that, reiterated on many different levels, mimics the relation between the mostly empty stadiums and the busy urban environments into which they are built. When the common spectator enters the stadium, half an hour or ten minutes before the kickoff for the game, he will see and be immediately attracted by the empty playing field, which is a promise for the imminent moment in which the teams will "take the field." It is through the utterly unsurprising and yet explosively exciting moment when the teams take the field that the spectators are conjured into their communal identity and agency.

After this inaugural scene, the central contrast shifts to the constantly repeated difference between slow movements (or stasis) and the speed and power typical of athletic performance. There is probably no other team sport that plays out more forcefully the potential of this structural element than American football. Preceding each play, two times eleven players stand in front of each other, like freeze-frames, drawing complicated forms on the field. What can follow, from the second that the center hands the ball to the quarterback to initiate a new play, is not completely covered by the contrast between the beautiful (offensive, negentropic) play or the destructive (entropic) powers of the defense. For American football also provides a type of situation where, after the seconds of the double freeze-frame, neither form nor chaos happen, the reasons for this "neither/nor" being "delayed game" or "offside." Following such a call, the players go back to the sidelines to talk the their coaches before they line up again. Nothing relevant for the game has happened meanwhile. And it is this impression of "nothingness" that matters.

For one might well speculate that players and spectators in a stadium jointly produce, on different levels, an embodiment of what Martin Heidegger, in the opening movement of his "Introduction to Metaphysics," identified as the one primordial philosophical question, that is the question of why there is something as opposed to nothing.[3] This question can well provoke existential vertigo to whoever dares to think through its possible consequences. But embodying a question is different from thinking it through and from exposing oneself to its existential impact. Most certainly players and spectators have no idea of what they may be embodying—and less an intention to do so. It is as if, in the sacred space of the stadium, they fulfilled a religious commandment for which neither words nor a theology is available.

4

In speaking and writing about sports from a historical angle, there is a tendency to overemphasize moments of repetition that suggest continuity, a tendency that probably comes from the—doubtlessly adequate—intuition that our participation in sports, both as athletes and as spectators, resonates with very basic and therefore metahistorical layers of human existence. Against this trend of focusing on historical invariables, it is important to highlight that, on the other hand, the circumstances under which such basic layers of our existence are being activated by sports make up for a history of astonishing discontinuity.[4] There were times, between Ancient Greek culture and today, where it would have been difficult to discover any phenomena resembling our present-day notion of athletics." None of those team sports, for example, whose incomparable popularity in the early twenty-first century tempts us to identify them with sports at large, existed before the mid-nineteenth century. The crowds that they attract, into stadiums and through the media, have been steadily growing over the past hundred years—and seem to continue to grow. Thus the idea becomes irrepressible [and perhaps even irrefutable] that the—at least quantitatively—triumphant history of team sports as spectator sports points to a new and important function of compensation, a function of compensation and secular re-enchantment that is—in a time when the Western process of secularization and disenchantment of the world (in the sense of Max Weber) may have reached a stage of close-to-perfection within our globalizing public sphere. For are there any phenomena left today that are allowed to be publicly nonrational and nonpragmatic?

We may also ask, in this context, why teams and their collectively produced epiphanies of form seem to fascinate us even more today than the most eminent players who are part of those teams and why we are moving away, if slowly, from that type of almost exclusive concentration on individual athletes that characterized Ancient Greek sports or the astonishingly popular world of professional boxing in England during the late eighteenth and early nineteenth century (today players who endlessly cultivate individual stardom, like the British soccer star David Beckham, clearly diminish their status within the world of athletics). A possible explanation might be that, in its present-day form, the re-enchantment provided by sports (and other phenomena) no longer appears to be a gift granted by the gods to athletes who are demigods but, probably, as an effect of the well-coordinated—perhaps even sacramentally coordinated—behavior of the many. It is difficult to predict where this development will take us. At any rate, sport, with its re-enchanting effects, has conquered a large proportion of the contemporary leisure world. As such, it stands in harsh contrast to a public and professional world that could hardly be more disenchanted. Should one take the most recent conquests of fashion (you can wear baseball caps and Nike sportswear in your office) as an indication for a future where sports will spill over into the rational dimension of our collective existence?

Today many of us still feel this beneficial effect of sports as compensating for things that we seem to lose and may already have lost irreversibly in the process of modern disenchantment, among them the effect of keeping open a place for the body in our existence. This would explain why so many sports fans (and I am certainly one of them) experience a both intense and vague gratitude toward their most admired heroes. It is a "vague" gratitude because we somehow know that former athletes or contemporary athletes "as private persons" cannot really be its addressees. Of course there are rare occasions that offer the possibility of (trying) to say, personally, "thank you, Mr. Jeter, for having been such an outstanding shortstop for the New York Yankees over so many years" or "dear Mr. Montana, I will never forget the soft accuracy of your touchdown passes." But not only is it (statistically at least) unlikely that our heroes will ever be thankful for such gratitude, let alone engage in a conversation with us. Above all, we feel that ours is a gratitude whose referent, quite literally, "transcends" the level of individuals and of individual conversations. In this sense ours is a gratitude similar to the gratitude that made the Greeks believe in spatial proximity to the gods as a condition for great athletic achievements. However, as so many of us have lost, for their private existence, the traditional religious horizons of transcendence, this gratitude gets deflected, so to speak, toward the world that we have. Gratitude for great athletic moments turns into gratitude for those things that we approve of, like, enjoy, and appreciate in our everyday lives. Being thankful for what we have does not necessarily make us "uncritical" and "affirmative." Although this exactly must be a fear that explains why so many intellectuals—even some intellectuals who love to watch or to practice sports—have such a hard time making their peace with it.

V. STEADY ADMIRATION
IN AN EXPANDING PRESENT

On Our New Relationship with Classics

While our relationship with classics has so far neither become a typical subject for exam questions nor appealed to literary supplements, many observations, some seemingly trivial, suggest that this relationship has altered—altered as it is experienced by educated readers, not as it is reflected in institutions, which are slower to respond to change. As yet we have no vocabulary to describe the shift; it has no name, no agenda—but it is certainly not restricted to the culture of any one particular nation. It is, indeed, the very diffuseness of this new relationship with classics that both reveals and obscures this novel dynamic.

Wherever developments of this nature have been perceived in the last three hundred years, two contrasting reactions have ensued with reflexive predictability. There have always been voices that celebrated a "return to the classics" as the inevitable triumph of absolute quality in a literal sense; something to be welcomed, as if the present were correcting itself, albeit too late. Yet others, with a slight sense of insecurity, have asked if retreat to classics is a symptom of the diminished vitality, even decadence, of the age.

We professional students of literature and the arts should have relegated such trite responses to the arena of dinner party repartee long ago, since they are no more than arbitrary postures, adopted uncritically. Indeed, we have an obligation to do so to those who finance us. The point is not to celebrate the latest development regarding the classics or to react with a frown. My alternative, in many respects more challenging, is to argue first and foremost that our new relationship with classics, still operating diffusely, has grown out of a change in our construction of time (I shall employ the word *chronotope* as a synonym here, though I am well aware that this usage does not convey all the nuances that students of Mikhail Bakhtin, the originator of this term, would insist upon). Time-forms, as we know from Edmund Husserl, shape the stage upon which we enact experience; including the context in which we read texts we have inherited on the pretext of their inherent merit.

My thesis only demands support because the transformation of our chronotope—which explains why our altered relationship with classics is so all-pervasive—has escaped the notice of the humanities. Those admirably complex terms *historical time* and *history* still—as, most prominently, Michel Foucault and Reinhart Koselleck have shown from such various points of departure—carry a range of reference that crystallized in the early nineteenth century. I argue that this range of reference no longer accurately characterizes the manner in which our experience is shaped in the present day. The transformation has caught us unawares; caught, indeed, everyone in the humanities unawares. So our new relationship with classics is in fact an important symptom of this new chronotope. Indeed, it is becoming clear that our relationship with authority, and not solely cultural authority, has undergone a transformation in tandem with our prevailing construction of time. For our new relationship with classics seems more irenic than it was in the era of historicism.

I will lay out my argument in five stages. First, I shall give some, as already stated, diffuse examples that tell of a new relationship with classics in our present. A brief reflection on the reform of the terms *classic* and *canon* between the eighteenth and nineteenth centuries will follow. This leads on to the third part of my argument, in which I compare the emergence of historicism after 1800 (and its implications for the terms *classic* and *canon*) with some of the reasons for its obsolescence in the third quarter of the twentieth century. Against this background it is possible to illuminate a new relationship with classics, not just—as I am arguing—in diffuse instances, but, first and foremost, in a new way of reading. Perhaps surprisingly, in the fifth part of my argument I look at how the situation differs from country to country. Lastly, I inquire whether, while our relationship with words such as *classic* and *canon* have changed through history, differences might not also have developed within nations.

1

It is often remarked that no brilliant thinkers have emerged among the intellectuals of recent decades. This is more obvious in Paris than anywhere else.

Less than three decades ago, an educated person who visited the city might have hoped to meet some of his contemporary intellectual heroes at a seminar or in a café (though the latter aspiration always accompanied a fairly predictable, romanticized notion of Paris). For at that time truly world-famous thinkers lived, taught, and wrote in Paris: the philosophers Gilles Deleuze, Jacques Derrida, and Jean-François Lyotard; the historians François Furet, Michel Foucault, and Jacques Le Goff; the semiotician who became a literary figurehead for a new movement, Roland Barthes; and Claude Lévi-Strauss—even then a kind of father figure—who was to outlive most of the others. There is certainly no lack of highly competent and productive humanities scholars in Paris today, but there are only a few figures that remain from that great period who give off any kind of aura—Michel Serres is one of them. This is surely symptomatic of our changed relationship with intellectual authority.

Simultaneously, we are more enthusiastic than every before about new (or recently augmented) editions of classic texts with extensive commentaries. The letters of Louis-Ferdinand Céline, which do not come close to matching the power of his literary prose, were a sensation in the French book market at the beginning of 2010. In Germany, above all, the apparently endless flood of anniversary celebrations has attained prodigious proportions, blazoning Johann-Peter Hebel's verse and blank face upon the pages of literary supplements and on the shelves of surviving bookshops. Whenever institutions offering funding dare to refuse applications for new editions of classics, they find themselves exposed to a storm of national indignation. Greater and lesser classics have appeared, not only as carefully edited texts but recently via widely researched and well-written biographies, too, which is all the more remarkable since, until recently, academics anathematized this genre. It may have been Stephen Greenblatt's biography of Shakespeare, as bold as it is lucidly speculative, that—after initial resistance—achieved an international breakthrough. Since then, certainly, no one in Germany has been surprised by a series of weighty accounts of Stephan George, followed by a history of reception that augments the biographical coverage; no one has been surprised by abundant accounts of Schiller's life, celebrating the 250th anniversary of his birth; indeed, people are not even surprised by a study of the life of the social historian Werner Conze, a scholar who was as unoriginal as he was opportunistic in his relationship to the Nazi rulers.

And all these books are read, discussed, and esteemed by a generation of amicable "young" scholars between the ages of twenty-five and fifty who are profoundly competent in narrow fields and thus avoid the oedipal conflicts that ensue from advancing provocative theses. What can the eminent ex-revolutionaries of my generation do but renounce both the well-maintained practice of "critical revision" and the ambitions of arcane seminars (e.g.,

"Cultural Difference in Alaska and the Problem of Frozen Traces") that we may pay homage to classics, saving as much face as possible? Instead of being stubborn, and finding myself ignored, I have acquired the habit of advertising one of my four lectures to college students and PhD students—in an economical program—under the bare names of classic Western writers: Jean Racine, Voltaire, Denis Diderot, and Gustave Flaubert; Friedrich Hölderlin, Heinrich von Kleist, Robert Musil, and Gottfried Benn; Lope de Vega, Calderón, García Lorca, and Luis Martín Santos. Success in teaching Kleist to undergraduates convinced me that this alteration to the degree course was more meritorious than one that conformed to academic convention. The listeners in Stanford enjoyed what they called "Kleist's linguistic mannerism": for instance, his description of the protracted cry of a robber who jumped into a stagecoach and was hit by the coachman's whip, which lets us interpret Kleist's lapidary conclusion to a letter of March 1792: "We happened upon this charming concert in Eisenach at 12 o'clock at night." The students also returned again and again to the mismatched footprints left behind by the village judge Adam's apprehensive trudging through the snow. Positively surprised by their fascination, when a little-known university in central Brazil invited me to give three lectures on Kleist I could not resist the temptation. More young people attended these lectures than any I had hitherto delivered, and they came to hear both the German original and an improvised Portuguese translation of Kleist quotes with which they were familiar. The suicide of Kleist and his lover Henrietta Vogel by the Wannsee, and his final letters written there, surprisingly (to me at least) became a favourite subject of theirs; in particular, the passage where Kleist likens the ascent of his and Henrietta's souls to that of two serene airships. There, in Vitoria da Conquista, a middle-sized town in the Brazilian state Bahia, if not before, it became clear to me that something fundamental had happened to our present's relationship with literary classics. At the time, though, this was not a change I could explain.

2

What exactly was and is the background against which we can we identify and describe a change in our relationship to the classics? In Germany no definition of the classic is more popular than Hans-Georg Gadamer's. By this definition, the "eminence" of these exceptional texts is founded on their enduring "immediate power to speak to us." Implicitly, then, classic texts strike us as possessing a paradoxical character, for Gadamer's historicist assumption is that as texts grow older their accessibility diminishes. Three issues become clear here: First, the term *classic*, used commonly until today, is a paradox. Second, its paradoxical form derives from the historicist assumption that the meaning of a text is dependent on its specific historical context. Third, this term *classic* flourishes, above all, in Germany, despite the relative unpopularity of the notion of a canon. For a canon is supposed to be timeless, and is therefore difficult to reconcile with a corpus of classics that are paradoxical anomalies.

If the relationship with classic texts (embodied in Gadamer's definition) was a cultural signature of the nineteenth and much of the twentieth century, its contradistinction to another definition of *classic*, popular until the eighteenth century, should be obvious. The article "Classique" in Diderot and d'Alembert's *Encyclopédie*, elaborated from the middle of the century of Enlightenment, lists a canon of texts from Greek and more especially Latin antiquities that—for no specified reason—are considered paradigmatic by virtue of their form and manifest wisdom. I shall not merely reiterate that the notion of a canon is necessarily weakened by the recognition that phenomena are susceptible to change over time and, consequently, to the progressive erosion of their claims to admiration. For the contrast between Gadamer's nineteenth-century definition and that of the *Encyclopédie* also reveals that circa 1800 a change must have taken place, which in two respects rendered the traditional synchronic definition of "classic" null and void. Since Reinhart Koselleck, as I have mentioned before, scholars in Germany have tended to associate important changes in the decades before and after 1800 with the metaphor of the "saddle period." For Koselleck himself, in the emergence of historicism we see something like the apparatus of thought of the saddle period—a period when many phenomena of change that he observed accumulated and converged.

3

Since I have argued that the institutionally dominant relationship with classics that predominated until recently was an outcome of historicism, I will briefly examine the latter's emergence at the beginning of the nineteenth century that we may establish whether the historicist chronotope entered a state of crisis in the twentieth century, and thus precipitated a change in our relationship with classics, and, if it did, why. The very emergence of a historically specific chronotope, which was to become so compelling and undisputed that for more than a century it was taken for "time" and "history" itself, can itself be seen as contingent upon the emergence of a historically specific mental attitude: second-order observation. By "second-order observer," I am referring to Niklas Luhmann's observer—an observer who in the act of observing, observes himself. Since human consciousness is always capable of second-order observation, which we would call self-reflection, we must specify that circa 1800 second-order observation had become prevalent in a particular social group. This is to say, from that date intellectuals (they were more frequently known by the French term *philosophe*) could not avoid observing themselves while observing the world. The perspectivist mode of delineating our experience was one direct consequence of this innovation. For a second-order observer discovers that the perspective of observation determines each of his experiences; and since he recognizes the infinity of possible perspectives, the second-order observer soon apprehends that for every object of experience there is a potential infinity of conceivable forms. A dizzying epistemological *horror vacui* ensues—abundantly apparent, for example, in Friedrich Schlegel's *Air of Reflection*. In the face of potentially *infinite* forms of experience and representation for every object of observation, how can one believe in the existence of an *ultimate* object of experience, identical with itself?

This problem would find a solution early in the nineteenth century that became the basis for the emergence of historicism. The solution was found in substituting a narrative manner of representing the world and ordering our experience for the mirrorlike structure. From the early nineteenth century, if you ask someone what Switzerland *is*, he will relate the history of Switzerland; those who seek to understand natural phenomena are urged to study evolutionary history. And when the young Hegel came to describe the nature of the spirit, he conceived his "phenomenology of the spirit" as a history. How could adopting a narrative mode for ordering our experience and representing the world fill the epistemological *horror vacui* unleashed by perspectivism? Precisely because narratives can absorb a plurality of representations of experience and link them to each other.

The historicist chronotope, wherein no phenomenon was immune to temporal change, soon unfolded on this foundation and made the permanent value of the classics, hitherto casually asserted, seem a paradox. One of the central endeavors of Reinhart Koselleck's work was to describe and historicize this chronotope, within which the past seems to be left behind by the passage of historical time, shedding its ability to give us our bearings. In historicist time the future appears as an open horizon of available possibilities. Between the past—which faded away forever behind its successor, the present—and the future, whose threshold lay before the next step, the present narrows to an "imperceptibly brief moment of transition" (as Charles Baudelaire put it in his *Le Peintre de la vie moderne* in 1857). The present as a mere moment of transition—as the place where the subject choses from the possibilities of the future based on past experience, adapted to the present—became an assumption for the Cartesian subject. This act of choosing is the central component of action. The particular nature of the present in the historicist chronotope therefore became a foundation and precondition of action.

In my experience the single most controversial element in my thinking (though it seldom provokes any real controversy) is my claim that the historicist chronotope no longer constitutes the matrix of assumptions that shape how we experience reality, though its discourse persists unaltered, even unto the present day. There is reason to regard the invective exchanged by intellectuals in the late seventies and early eighties who suddenly sought to be "postmodern," and their opponents who determined to persevere with the modernist project, as symptomatic of the rapidly shifting chronotope. This is not to say that the new chronotope should be named a postmodern one or that the postmodern faction should claim a victory. What is significant, rather, is that in the course of this debate—which seems to us, in retrospect, excessively acrimonious—and, more precisely, in Jean-François Lyotard's pamphlet *La condition postmoderne*, a central premise of the historicist mentality was rendered problematic with lasting consequences. Above all, Lyotard sought to criticize the claims of "great" totalizing historical metanarratives to represent absolute truth. Might not, Lyotard asks, a potentially infinite number of competing historical narratives supersede dominant institutionalized narratives? Thus the narrative mode of representation was challenged as a solution to the problem of perspectivism and the basis of the historicist mentality and was soon abandoned. In the decades leading up to our present, a new—still nameless—chronotope was established as a premise for our experience of reality in the place of the historicist mentality. Instead of constantly leaving our pasts behind us, in the new chronotope we are inundated by memories and objects from the past. Time no longer erodes the "direct power to speak to us" of classics. Instead of transporting us onto a wide horizon of possibilities, today the future appears intimidating in many respects. And so, between the threatening future and the past in which we are immersed, an ever expanding present has become of that "imperceptibly brief moment of transition." It is at least possible that recourse to the notion of a canon might easily reintegrate the classics as a component within this pluralistic sphere of simultaneity. If it is indeed true that the Cartesian subject was situated epistemologically within the narrow present of the historicist mentality, then it is unsurprising, in this new ever expanding present, when we search for more nuanced alternatives of human self-reference to the Cartesian "subject."

In our new chronotope the relentless dynamic of historical movement has weakened and, in any case, the momentum of temporal procession has stalled in the meantime. That makes our encounters with classics more relaxed because their power to speak to us directly is no longer threatened—nor is it peculiarly theirs. In the new chronotope the documents of the past are present with truly confusing variety and require not so much preservation from amnesia as infiltration. And yet we hesitate to follow John of Salisbury of the twelfth century, for whom contemporary thinkers, though they be mere "dwarfs on the shoulders of giants," could inevitably see further than their more eminent predecessors—perhaps because classics are now so immediately accessible to us. A more relaxed relationship does not necessarily become a more intellectually and aesthetically productive relationship.

In the new chronotope we seek to replace the traditional Cartesian subject and we are therefore more alive to the greater complexity of human existence than that suggested by the *cogito*. In the new chronotope the authority and hierarchical power of the state (and perhaps not only the power of the state) have diminished—in contrast to the nightmares of boundless state power so powerfully articulated in novels of the mid-twentieth century such as *1984* and *Brave New World*. In our quotidian existence we live in laterally linked webs, not hierarchical relations of dependence. The English language has responded with a tendency to replace the term *government* with *governance*. All this may issue from a new chronotope in which an inhibited future has made the possibility of *practically* molding the future—the possibility of a politics of practice—more challenging. At the same time, the weakness of the practical paradigm is more openly evident in a longing for charisma and direction that must also have effects in the world of culture.

4

These still somewhat tentative observations of our new chronotope's consequences, clearly manifesting themselves today, make the suggestion that our relationship with classics has changed plausible and historically well founded. Against this background, I would like to pose the narrower (and in its narrowness essentially empirical) question whether a change in our attitude to classics is expressed in new approaches and attitudes to the reading of texts. I shall offer some observations, the first of which is concerned with ways of reading the classics. My generation grew up with an intellectual commitment to mistrust classics in all their forms. By contrast, it was widely suspected that admiration for classics was, in all respects, merely proof of conformity to the ideologies of their, or our, world. We aspired to become specialists in subverting the classics. This prejudice and the ambition it engendered have long been absent, both among the generation of nicely competent young scholars today and the youngest generation of students, who accept the basic premise that reading classics pays dividends, particularly with relation to the present. One then attempts self-examination with a new steadiness to understand where such dividends might arise in particular cases. That growing interest among so many who heard my Kleist lectures in Vitoria da Conquista, to which I referred a moment ago, was in this respect as typical an experience as it was eccentric; it changed my view on the status of classics today irreversibly. These listeners had to penetrate Kleist for the first time to discover how much his death wish fascinated them. Following Heidegger, they came to practise a "piety of reading" and were, I hope, rewarded.

But, above all, I believe that today we read classics less politically than even a quarter of a century ago—and experience the texts instead, to bring in a conflicting term, from an *existential* perspective. We no longer relate words, images, and scenes from classical texts, to the problems of "contemporary society" or even to the problems of "humanity itself." Instead, we relate them to the manifold eventualities and challenges encountered in individual lives: not in relation to *our own* lives, but rather in relation to challenges *typical* of life, close to the hearts of many readers. That the traditional Cartesian "subject" has been challenged as a central model for human self-reference renders the new existential imperative still more acute. Such a change in readers' perspectives can partially explain the allure and even the academic rehabilitation of the biographical genre. For the biographies of literary figures do not simply attempt to locate the origins of the themes and forms of their texts. An inquiry into the genesis of themes and forms can be turned on its head and then becomes another handicap for "applying" texts (following Gadamer's usage). A reader who understands how Kleist's longing to die arose will be able to discover more relationships between this dimension of Kleist's texts and specific questions, which may change his own views—and, beyond that, perhaps suggest the beginnings of protracted paths of argument and reflection. Incidentally, the most important justification for collecting and reappraising forewords and afterwords, as the Marbacher archive (the German national archive and the national museum for literature) does so energetically, is that it makes them available for such existential applications.

It is possible that the level on which we apply the classics—one is tempted to say the ontological level—is currently shifting to an existential domain revealed and informed by biography. One can certainly ascribe no ability to enrich life, as my German teacher used to promise in my last year at grammar school, to Kleist's *Farewell Letters* or the traces left behind by the village judge Adam in the snow. Or, less paradoxically, perhaps the occasionally praised "hermeneutic logic of question and answer" acquires fresh purchase over our new way of reading classics. Resurrecting intense experiences is what fascinates us today, even in philology, which has suddenly become fascinating again. Rather than posing and answering concrete questions, our semiotics of aesthetic philosophy concerns itself with the emotions of the reader; we concentrate immediately on dimensions such as "elegy" "melancholy," "tragedy" or "fate"; we want to get to the bottom of the "dialects of emotion"—and temporal signs of "precipitancy" or "irreversible departure" familiarized by Karl Heinz Bohrer. Even the striking contrast (to play on Kleist one last time) between a failed life and the overwhelmingly lovely artifacts it leaves behind can become a source of existential provocation and literary consolation today.

5

Setting aside our altered way of reading classic texts, we would expect canonical bodies of texts to be more readily established and more apparent in the new chronotope than they were under the reign of the historicist mentality. Should we actualize this potential and build—under very specific circumstances—a national canon? My view, though it lacks clear conviction or particular passion, is probably not. Probably not, because the texts that we call classic today certainly cannot impart the foundations we think of if we talk—wisely or unwisely—of demanding familiarity with a national culture in all members of society. It is unrealistic to seek in Faust some means to access the German identity of today—and, sadly, knowledge of such texts is not especially helpful to attaining social recognition or advancement (unlike in England, France, and perhaps even the United States). I am also inclined to oppose the project of elaborating a national canon because such an exclusively national focus has for a long time ceased to correspond with the habits of those educated people who commonly abstain from reading altogether. Looking at the German book market, we see an emphasis on ambitious translations of classic texts from other national literatures with extensive commentaries—only recently, new editions of Miguel de Cervantes's *Don Quixote* and Stendhal's *Le rouge et le noir* appeared. A few years ago, a new English edition of the *Man Without Qualities* won Robert Musil recognition among American readers as one of the great authors of the twentieth century for the first time. Of course, such examples and tendencies mean neither that we can exclude texts valued as "classic" in certain national cultures today nor that, with the exception of certain wistful academic imaginings, a developing global canon is really perceptible.

That notwithstanding, there are distinct national differences in the literary canon that have evidently persisted almost unchallenged, though literary theorists have never dwelt on it—perhaps it has in fact escaped their attention. It was not particularly surprising—but still profoundly striking, at least for me as a student of Romance languages educated in Germany—to discover that to establish a panel discussion with French Germanists on the subject of the classic and the canon requires almost infinite explicit clarifications. Such hitherto neglected national differences, with which I am concerned, are therefore differences in the assumptions and emphases with which one reads in different national cultures.

Until the present day, the prescriptive authority of the classics over spoken and written language has been nowhere so unchallenged as in France—the Académie française and Comédie française spring to mind—where the legitimate existence of a canon has never been questioned in principal—unlike in Germany. No single individual has been so comprehensively canonized in any national literature as William Shakespeare and his oeuvre in the Anglosphere. Shakespeare's unmatched position also explains why "drama" occupies so prominent a position in the teaching of literature and literary scholarship. It is difficult to imagine that a person might complete secondary education without at some point playing a Shakespeare role and reciting his lines. On the other hand, no national canon of classics has been so narrowly defined, so undisputed, and so chronologically removed as Dante, Boccaccio, and Petrarch, the "three jewels" of Italian literature. That might be because, until now, in no other culture has the literary canon and the language shaped by its authors become so manifest a part of the national identity as in Italy. If we may speak of a national literary canon in Japan, two main theatrical genres are central: *Noh* and *Kabuki*, which originated in the seventeenth and eighteenth centuries. Yet it is not the authors of drama that exemplify this canon so much as the great thespian dynasties, on whose members the state has conferred the status of "national treasure." A notable peculiarity of the Spanish literary canon is apparent in the status that the protagonists of its texts have attained, rivaling that of classic authors, to the extent that protagonists have superseded their creators—and sometimes even stand in their place. In the middle of the Plaza de España in Madrid there is a sculpture of Don Quixote and Sancho Panza, not one of Miguel de Cervantes.

And what is the distinctive tone of the German literary canon? It betrays itself in intensive reflection on the assumptions and values that have informed the reading of classic texts in German culture for 250 years, possibly owing to the vicissitudes of history. For German purposes it has almost always been difficult to locate and claim a direct route to classics. Precisely this unusual quality has generated the sometimes rather exaggerated impartiality so popular among nonprofessional readers that Marcel Reich-Ranicki deploys when he writes about his favorite texts as "classics." Yet the German inclination to intense reflection seems to survive him, and even more complex alterations in our relationship with classic texts, that the new chronotope has set in motion.

VI. INFINITE AVAILABILITY

About Hypercommunication (and Old Age)

We have more opportunities to communicate than ever before in the history of Homo sapiens. This is the elementary fact that I am referring to with the word *hypercommunication*, and I refrain from saying that hypercommunication is either a good or a bad thing. Now, the frequency with which we talk to other persons face-to-face, that is, in mutual physical presence, has most likely not increased—but it has probably also not dramatically declined during the past decades. If we have more opportunities to communicate than ever before, in the sense of conducting interactions based on the use of natural languages, then this increase is clearly a function of technical devices whose effects neutralize the consequences of physical as well as sometimes also temporal distance. Telephone and electronic mail, radio, gramophone, and television are such arrays. Of course there is a basic structural difference setting apart, on the one side, telephone and electronic mail, as media that allow for exchange and mutual impact and, on the other side, the more "asymmetrical" media like radio, gramophone, and television where only persons at the—irreversibly—receiving end have a perception of those individuals who initiate communication without ever getting immediate feedback.

But the most fascinating electronic communication tools are the ones that produce the physical impression of an interaction at distance, although there is but one body involved. Different from the spectators who, particularly in the eighteenth century, were intrigued by those chess-playing "machines," we know for a fact that there is no employee of our bank or of our airline involved when we use, for example, an automatic teller machine (ATM) or when we check in at the airport by using a screen, nor are we really deceived by the mostly female voices that lend spatial presence to the navigation system in our car. And yet we often act—and we like to act—as if a real person was involved on the other side. Who, quite honestly, has never called that navigation lady "a bitch"? And who has not been pleased or put off, at some point, by the polite language, the efficiency, and sometimes the design of those airline screens helping us to get ready for the next flight?

My opening sentence, then, presupposing that we are inclined to subsume all these different kinds of technically facilitated "interaction" under the concept of communication. Many of them, like the ATM around the corner, the check-in device at the local airport, or the program at the customer service number of your Mastercard, simply replace former institutions and situations of face-to-face interaction. They are never exactly the same as the structures preceding them, but the differences between the real person (formerly) and the electronic function (today) is obviously meant to remain at a level that avoids confusion. I also think that this is the disappointingly banal reason why all these new variet-ies of techno-permeated communication have in the end not inspired theories as earthshaking and grandiose as some of us had originally hoped for (remem-ber with what excitement we once read Jean Baudrillard, Vilém Flusser, or Paul Virilio?). Evidently, we are far from completely controlling, say, the addictive temptations of e-mail. But this is not so terribly different from people having spent more time than they could afford, for millennia, in pointless face-to-face conversations.

The innovation brought about by those devices, therefore, does not lie in any specific features through which they copy or exceed the possible performance of a human person—it lies in their ubiquity. Without any doubt, the number of cash machines we can use now, twenty-four hours a day and seven days per week, beats the highest number of bank employees ever hired and paid in order to provide customers with cash. Airlines will spread their welcoming presence more widely throughout the airport buildings, with those touch screens, than they ever could while they were limited to a coherent segment of space for check-in. Whatever we need seems to be more available than before through electronic communication. But, whether we want this or not, it is true that we, i.e., those who use ATMs and touch screens, become more available too.

At my university, I have the enviable privilege of a small office in the middle of the library whose occupant (and I am the present occupant) is supposed to remain anonymous. Among other things, this office, different from my other office on campus, where I see students and colleagues, was meant to protect me or, rather, to set me at a distance from the invasiveness of electronic communication (and any other type of communication that I do not actively choose), like the private space of my home where I don't do e-mail either. I used to take care of the several hundred e-mail messages that I receive on a normal working day during deliberately limited hours of the morning and the evening in my official campus office, while the time in the carrel and the working time at home were exclusively dedicated to reading and writing. What, naively, I had not taken into account was the strange agency effect of my laptop—my laptop that I had meant to use exclusively as a writing instrument, something like a functionally much improved electronic typewriter. One day, to my surprise, the laptop screen let me know that, thanks to an upgrading of the library buildings to the level of electronically sensitive spaces, it was now making available all the messages in my carrel that I had wanted to reserve for the computer in my other on-campus office, making me thus available too to the world—very much against my intention. From the perspective of my personal work and my subjective well-being, this excessive availability was vulnerability. I know that universal availability is generally considered to be the main effect and the unconditional value of electronically provided hypercommunication. It has been celebrated as a democratic value, but it is one of those democratic values that Nietzsche would have associated with a situation of slavery. Whoever is electronically available must break all democratic rules of politeness to avoid e-mail addiction and e-mail victimage. It is considered rude—and it is therefore difficult—not to communicate. Beside that, availability undoes all hierarchies and social differences. Pretty much every day, I receive some messages in which students tell me that they have a real necessity to talk to me, that they would consider it a great favor and privilege if I set up a meeting with them—and then they continue by letting me know the time and the electronic addresses under which they will be "available." How impossibly old-fashioned is it if I regularly feel that in this type and under these conditions of interaction it should be exclusively my privilege to be "available" or not?

1

Vis-à-vis all these electronic gadgets, vis-à-vis hypercommunication as their effect, and even vis-à-vis the very trendy academic attempts at theorizing them both, I take a position resembling the attitude of those fifteenth-century monks, scribes, and scholars who feared, criticized, and finally even actively rejected the printing press. While I do not literally believe that electronic communication devices are the devil's work and will have a generally deteriorating effect on culture at large, I give in, quite often, to the temptation of describing them as agents and symptoms of intellectual decadence and I try to know as little about them as I can possibly afford. I have learned, proudly, that my university cannot legally oblige me to change office computers each time that we are offered the opportunity of doing so—and I relish the shock that some of my colleagues go through when they realize that the size of the computer screen in my office is three and a half technological generations behind what they consider to be standard. But I doubt they could explain to me in a really convincing way why it is so much better to have a very large screen.

Nor have I ever believed in that teleological faith according to which we make inventions when we most need them. Of course this can happen, randomly or as the result of an intense effort, but it clearly is the exception. Oftentimes—and perhaps even most frequently—new technical devices or cultural practices emerge independently of the collective needs in their environment, and even whether, once invented, they will be broadly assimilated by a society or not not only hinges upon their practical value but may well be motivated, for example, by their aesthetic appeal. There was no real pragmatic "need" for radio and television, for example, but radio immediately and television after a long period of incubation ended up profoundly transforming not only our sphere of leisure. Once such innovations have become institutionalized, their existence and their presence appear irreversible, and it is in this sense that Niklas Luhmann called them evolutionary achievements. Such an optimistic-sounding phrase hides the experience that many of the innovations to which we refer with it end up positioning humans in situations of dependence and victimhood that greatly reduce their range of agency and efficiency. Ironically enough, some Silicon Valley companies were among the first to realize that they lost billions of dollars, year after year and with a sharp increase, due to the addiction that prevented their employees from working in front of a computer screen without checking its e-mail functions every few minutes.

At any event, the so-called evolutionary achievements inevitably add up, and by adding up they produce the impression of a trajectory we can then interpret, in a Hegelian mood, as "historically necessary." Nobody will ever be able to prove or to disprove the historical necessity of a fact after the fact—and within this unmarked space of uninhibited speculation it has been one of the more exciting hypotheses to say, as, for example, the French paleontologist André Leroi

Gourhan did, that civilization, with technology as its core, may have replaced the biological (?) energy that used to propel the evolution of our species and this happened at a time when the biological evolution of humankind has greatly slowed down and may indeed have come to a standstill.

In this technical, cultural, and intellectual environment, all I have—very modestly—been hoping for during the past ten years (and I am now sixty-one years old) is that certain objects and situations that I grew up with, and which, therefore, belong to my being-in-the-world, will not disappear under the pressure of the latest evolutionary achievements. I am also claiming the (moral?) right to be exempted from the obligation of embracing each and every technical innovation. Not necessarily because I have profound reasons for my resistance against so much communication, but because its forms and phenomena just hit me too late in life, perhaps only by a few years, to ever assimilate them all in a comfortable way. I know how ridiculous it would be if I pretended that I am trying to slow down and even to stop a historical drift. I just want polite tolerance when I give lectures without using PowerPoint and I want a chance to convince my students that it might be an opportunity for them if I do not give in to their regular demand of "using more visuals" in my courses. Theirs, much more than mine, is an everyday world of moving images, so that it might be enriching, for both sides, to be confronted with this difference. At some point, perhaps, I will end up being convinced that the gap between my own communicative style and that of my students has grown to a degree that is seriously problematic. This will be the day for me to change my approach to teaching—or, more likely, to retire. But I refuse to make the effort of laboriously adapting myself to an environment that I do not feel comfortable with and that makes me look inept. For example, there are too many potential virtues—and even democratic values—in distance learning to ever actively fight it. And yet I know that my university will have disappeared the day we are no longer allowed to sit around a table with our (not too many) students. I also know that I would not be very successful and would certainly not look good if I tried to take notes, from a lecture or discussion, with a laptop on my knees. And I believe that this is also the case for most of the colleagues my age who claim, unconvincingly, to have been early champions of the electronic revolution (I recently saw one of them drop the laptop from his knees three times in one hour of discussion). What I most fear when I use communication technologies that I have not grown up with is an embarrassing lack of grace in my behavior. In other words: the strongest reason for my anti-electronic attitude is an anticipated aesthetic judgment about myself.

2

A full repertoire exists with figures and configurations that are emblematic of a world that has filled its empty zones with technology-facilitated opportunities to communicate, and, somehow strangely, these figures and configurations strike me as emblems of solitude and isolation. The most salient among them is the lonesome walker who, at first glace, seems to speak to himself, often with great emphasis, particular expressivity, and also quite loudly, and thus appears to perfectly fit one of the traditional images of the fool as "he who talks to himself." As we all know, the problem, here, lies in the eye of the beholder. For as soon as we discover, around the person's neck or behind her ear, the trace of an electronic communication device, she turns from an uncanny figure of foolishness into somebody who is privileged to spend time with a beloved one, say, on her way to work. Now let us assume that the beloved one, in the specific case of the lonesome walker-talker whom we are watching, is her lover. In such a case they may well use electronic communication, during their working day, to allude to moments of erotic intensity that they remember from the night before and which they look forward to. Such an exchange will draw its specific excitement from establishing a bubble of ecstatic privacy closely surrounded by the most formal and sometimes even most public business relations. I can still remember that late afternoon when, driving back to our house, the road was blocked by all the books and furniture that the wife of a colleague had thrown through the window after she had read the daily mail to his two extramarital lovers (who didn't know of each other: one an undergraduate student and one a senior woman colleague)—a mail that he, by confusion, had addressed to his spouse and to the provost of the university. Possible Freudian interpretations apart, interpretations, for example, about an "unconscious desire for confession" coming through in such an accident, I believe that it is the dangers of contiguity that lend a background of erotic charge to the solitude of electronic communication.

Nothing less erotic, by contrast, than those mails and cell phone calls to spouses or relatives that more than half the passengers on a normal flight feel the irresistible urge to make in the very first moment—right after touchdown—they are allowed to do so. This reaction is no different from smokers grabbing their pack of cigarettes as soon as they arrive at one of the few remaining spaces in our world where cigarette smoke is not banned; both are symptoms of addiction. Nobody waiting for us at the airport really needs to know, again, that our plane has landed, given that there is a multiplicity of screens, in the waiting area, that provide the exact same information. Nor do they need to know, ten minutes later, that we are still waiting for the suitcase at the baggage claim and that, four minutes later, it is in sight. By the time the arriving passenger embraces his wife, it may feel that he already had arrived "too much," that his body, which he now adds to the already present mind and voice, has no existential place.

To be a body-less and space-less medium and thus never to turn into an ecological burden gives an aura of political correctness to electronic communication, at least in the perception of those who aggressively use it—and this surely is a surplus even over the always praised "convenience" of electronic devices. When you ask for hard copies to be airmailed or fedexed because your eyes suffer from reading long texts on a screen or because you want to forego the ordeal of printing endless manuscripts, you will often face the threat of a refusal that gives itself the triumphant aura of ecological responsibility. For who would be so courageous and selfish as to care more about his own remaining eyesight than about the remaining trees? Finally, there is this other aura, the ultimate aura, produced by the line, toward the end of some electronic messages: "Sent from my Blackberry." The aristocratic design of this device, the tone conveyed by the four words quoted, and the knowledge that his Blackberry is the one body part of President Barack Obama that gives him credibility as being contemporaneous and even futuristic, these and other factors may come together in producing an effect of hierarchy in the communication with Blackberry users. Are they perhaps those happy few who let us know that they are graciously available—but that their availability should not be taken advantage of? Whenever I receive a message saying: "Sent from—somebody's—Blackberry," I feel that I am at the lower end of a regal message and that, rather than respond, I should wait for subsequent messages—or even orders.

3

Not only do I have so many more opportunities then ever before to communicate, which, if I only managed to control myself, might well be a blessing, these opportunities also make instantly available to me a large portion of those humans whose segments of lifetime overlap with mine, among them many whom I actively care about, like the two of my four children living in Europe and my only granddaughter. What do I complain about, except about the victim status that comes from having to be so terribly available myself? My answer is that hypercommunication erodes those contours that used to give form, drama, and flavor to my everyday. Here is an example. Whenever I agree to give a reasonably well-paid lecture these days ("reasonably well paid" meaning that the organizers, on whichever grounds, attribute a certain importance to it), I am being asked, early on, to provide a title and a summary of non-negligible length, for the purpose of (mostly electronic) advertising. Almost at the same time, somebody will demand that I make available a manuscript of my lecture to those who, for one reason or the other, will not be able to attend. On the day of the lecture at the very latest, somebody will want me to sign a form giving my consent to the production of a recording. All this is partly flattering (one feels "in demand") and partly nerve-racking (especially for somebody who relies, for lectures, on scarce handwritten notes, i.e., notes that normally are the very condensed result of a long reflection process). But, taken together, all these interventions tend to flatten those contours and hard transitions that used to give a specific event character to lectures in the preelectronic age. Who attends a lecture, thus the new ideal, should to do so in rereading or relistening to an already known text and who chooses not to attend should definitely not lose the possibility of reading it or to listening to it at a later date. As we are so eager to make our consciousness universally available, we end up spreading thin our physical presence: nothing is ever absolutely new any more and nothing is ever irreversibly over.

If hypercommunication levels the excitement coming from the discontinuity implied in any beginning, it also smooths the pain or the tragedy of ending and separation. Your girlfriend may be eight hundred (or six thousand) miles away, but, in contrast to when I was young and the telephone was both very expensive and even more unreliable, there is the consoling privacy of Facebook (if it produces "privacy" at all, I have to ask, admitting that I have never used Facebook). The price to be paid for this palliative effect is that our ideas, our imaginations, and our daydreams are each time less where we are with our bodies. You see people meeting for dinner at gorgeous places on Friday night, only to be lured away by a ringing cellphone or by an SMS message right after sitting down. And when they arrive at the meeting that they are now coordinating, their minds will again be ahead of their bodies.

Together with the contours of eventness and with the existential contrasts between presence and absence, private and public, we may also lose, with so many "sites" juxtaposed on the Web, a sense for what matters and what does not. Of course, some sites receive many more "hits" than others—but the hope that electronic sites of all kinds will ever provide the physical and intellectual intensity of a discussion in physical copresence has long vanished. Has anybody ever seen a truly good debate in electronic form, a debate where mutual argumentative resistance turns into mutual inspiration and new ideas? While it is difficult to explain why electronic discussions produce, at best, spiritual mediocrity, we all know that this is the case—inevitably somehow. Even on my best friend's Web site I can only be alone, and what I may feel there, as a hint of closeness, never transcends the closeness of a tourist or that of a voyeur. Is there anything more pathetic than those tens of thousands (I fear hundreds of thousands) of blogs that are being written with such self-importance—and will forever remain unread (for good reasons, I want to add)? On the Web, to eliminate the risk of catching a cold is balanced, at least for me, by the loss of the chance to be moved to tears—not to speak of the senses of touch, taste, and smell that must remain unaffected.

4

But what do I really want, what is my—practical—ideal? One strong wish that I have is for the continuation of that "philosophical reading group" as which we—about thirty faculty and students—meet at Stanford every Thursday night for a good two or three hours, with the aim of discussing, in small segments, just one philosophical book (mostly classics) over a period of ten weeks. Regardless of whether the text chosen for a certain trimester is close to my own working agenda or not, the energy of that reading group has become my intellectual lifeline. But there is no doubt that, for all its intensity, our philosophical reading group has lost, in recent years, important participants to an ever growing number of other workshops whose emergence the electronic gesture of juxtaposition seems to foster.

I also have a much more romantic, archaic, and unrealistic memory of a moment I loved, a memory that I am obsessed with, a recollection of a world that was never mine and must by now be gone for ever. About fifteen years ago a former student of mine took me to a small town in Louisiana called New Iberia, with the purpose of visiting a former plantation that boasted of being "the home of the first pair of blue jeans." On our way back to the car, I believe, we walked by a bayou where two very old black men stood looking into the water. After a few minutes, one of these two very old black men turned to us to explain, very politely and in a French whose sounds were conjured up from the late seventeenth century, that alligators up to three feet long were very tasty and tender, whereas the flesh of four-foot-long alligators was tough and impossible to eat. Five or six years later, I returned to beautiful New Iberia with my family. For the second time in my life, I saw the first pair of blue jeans and I again walked by the bayou where, I swear, I saw those same two very old black men again who had not aged and told us, with the very same words as the first time, what they felt my family and I should know about the gastronomic qualities of three- and of four-foot-long alligators. No event in my entire life had clearer contours, and no experience is more present in my memory than that double communication with two very old black men at New Iberia, Louisiana.

5

We cannot avoid "having" a body that we occasionally use and whose effects we more frequently bracket—but we are fast losing the ability to "be" a body, that is, the ability to let the body be an enhancing condition of our existence. Nothing, by contrast, is more Cartesian in the sense of body free than all the different kinds of electronic communication, nothing is more seamlessly connectable with our consciousness than they are, and nothing is more withdrawn from the dimension of space. This is the reason why electronically based hypercommunication brings to its insuperable completion the process of modernity, as the process in which the human subject as pure consciousness has emancipated itself from and triumphed over the human body and all other kinds of *res extensae*. Not that there was much left to be conquered, for consciousness, at least in mainstream Western culture, before the first chip was invented and before the first personal computers were sold. But, in order to become perfect and, above all, irreversible, the democratically enslaving principle of universal availability needed the reduction of human existence through the computer screen. Since within this dimension, contours, discontinuities, and borders tend to vanish, we now spend most of our lives in the invariably same position, i.e., in front of the eternal computer screen. We are there while we fulfill our professional duties, when we communicate with our beloved ones, and, most of all, when the threat arises of being alone. For we have traded the pain of solitude caused by physical absence for the everlasting half-solitude of those who make themselves infinitely available.

Everything melts together; everything is "fusion." But in spite of all the talking about it, I cannot see any "mixed realities" that would deserve this name. It may all be my fault, i.e., a consequence of my mostly deliberate old-fashionedness, if I insist that a sensual perception will always remain separate from a concept or from a thought. What seems to be new is that, most of the time, we focus neither on the one nor on the other side of this spectrum, which must be the reason why our new pride is based on the particular type of alertness required in order to manage an existence of complex simultaneities. While I was writing this text, I occasionally checked incoming e-mails and, as it is mid-July, I also just saw who won today's stage of the Tour de France (it was, to my great American regret, Alberto Contador from Spain). This predominant situation of early twenty-first-century human realities converges with the impression that the "imperceptibly short" present of the historicist construction of time, that is, the construction of time that emerged in the early nineteenth century, which became so dominant that we tended to confuse it with time in and of itself, that the imperceptibly short present characteristic of the historicist chronotope has now been replaced by an ever broadening present of simultaneities. In today's electronic present, there is neither anything "from the past" that we need to leave behind nor anything "from the future" that could not be made present by simulated anticipation.

Some of us old ones feel that this is simply too much—and that, at the same time, it is not enough presence. If the process of modernity has largely been a process of disenchantment, we have now written Rational Reenchantment on our revolutionary banners. But I am fully aware that this is but another Gray Panthers' revolution.

IN THE BROAD PRESENT

The ways the horizons of the future and the past are experienced and connect with an ever broader present give form to the as yet unnamed chronotope within which globalized life in the early twenty-first century occurs. "On the outside," the form of this new chronotope makes it different from other chronotopes, especially that of "historical consciousness." "On the inside," it dictates the conditions under which human behavior finds its constitutive structures and experiences. The view follows—to be historically precise—Edmund Husserl's intuition that "time is the form of experience." The contours of life in the present (which differs fundamentally from that of "historical time") have hardly been sketched at all from a perspective that does not focus on individual phenomena. I can by no means claim to have done so here in a way that is complete—or even elegant. My aim is more modest. On the following pages I will bring together observations from the six chapters of this book; perhaps this will yield a first glimpse, a few beginning speculations, about life in the new present.

The fragmentary account of our broad present consists of four oscillations, which certainly—and the point bears repeating—are neither exhaustive nor synonymous with its totality. I consider oscillation to be constitutive of the present and therefore I believe that it will be productive for our understanding to retain this figure of thought, should, one day, the project of accounting for the whole of the broad present be carried to completion. The dramatic polarity between the everyday, on the one hand, and the growing—if largely reactive—insistence on the demands of presence, on the other, shape our present. This polarity creates the force field in which, today, our lives are set. The opposites that compose it cannot be "mediated" or "resolved"—what would the "synthesis" of reflexivity-at-a-distance and participatory intensity even mean?

I believe "oscillation" is key because, at any given moment, one can only occupy one of the two sides in a field. From one moment to the next, the absolute freedom to change position exists, and it is impossible to forget the other pole and even to resist its attraction. This may—at least in part—explain the intransitive mobilization that characterizes the present, which threatens to overwhelm us and, as a general rule, bends the linearity of our projects and actions into an inefficient circularity. Finally, it is worth emphasizing once more that the freedom to follow impulses of movement in different directions, which we do in fact enjoy, does not entail the freedom to select objects of attention at will—nor, to be sure, to carry projects to term. The broad present always directs us to determinate objects; this does not mean, in principle at least, that we may not be genuinely interested in and passionate about them.

To begin with—and here lies the first of the four oscillations to be discussed—the broad present points us (more, perhaps, than ever before in the history of humanity) to Planet Earth, the site of the very condition for our individual and collective survival. A necessary reference to the planet is no longer just the consequence of the sober mood that spread rapidly in the second half of the twentieth century, when projects for the "conquest of space" became more grounded. Since then, it has been accepted that the conditions favoring life on the planet will not endure. Consequently, a new—as it were, microscopic—turn to the things-of-the-world and their care has developed, both as a scientific and as a political task, but also as an increasingly intensive habitus of everyday existence.

Opposed to this necessity and passion for proximity to things stands an unrevised philosophical skepticism, which, after a prehistory lasting centuries, found its canonical intellectual expression in the so-called linguistic turn. The observations we make possess certainty only in the languages we use (and, one might add, in the introspection that consciousness affords). Therefore, the reasoning goes, shared "knowledge" about objects outside language and consciousness always stands under suspicion of merely being a "social construction of reality," which implies that it is impossible ever to arrive at what is "really real." The dramatic potential within the first point of oscillation becomes clear if one sees in this philosophical position (which, in terms of the consequences it holds for our lives, is harmless enough in itself) a parallel to the merging of "real" and "financial" markets, which most specialists consider the root of the financial crisis that has gripped the world since 2008—if one, that is, identifies a parallel between a philosophical style that takes stock only of language and consciousness on the one hand and the exchange of and speculation in "derivatives" on the other. Far-reaching economic crises impose the delay of ecological and political measures and interventions—with consequences for the sustainability of the planet that might prove irreversible. No obvious alternative stands ready, since even specialists do not know how a new economy might begin without soon returning to this kind of speculation.

The second oscillation involves the bodily dimension of our existence. In an everyday work environment that, in more and more professions, is set in front of a computer screen, our bodies have become obsolete in many functional regards. At the same time, however, the discourses of cultural criticism lay claim to definite bodily rights, and the new, broad present also accords them a position of epistemological importance. One aspect of the second point of oscillation concerns a tendency, which one encounters particularly in European societies, to leave responsibility for, and power over, individual bodies entirely to the state. Expectations of state-organized and financed care for the sick and elderly literally know no limit. (It is impossible to convince European intellectuals that there might be people who, against their own economic interests, do not wish to yield the care of their health to the state.) Given de facto pacifism and widespread initiatives for civil protest, there is remarkably little resistance to compulsory military service (which, in most national contexts, evidently serves the purpose of minimizing youth unemployment). Most astounding of all, perhaps, is the fact that it is still the norm in Western legal systems to count suicide a violation of the law. Clearly, the body and life do not stand at the disposition of the individual subject.

At the other end of the second field of oscillation—and here the demands are more radical than ever before—it is assumed that the individual body, as an object of play and experimentation, is freely available to the individual—and that it is only right that this be the case. The limits on legitimate sexuality, we believe, should be determined only by the tolerance and consent of the adults involved. Clearly at odds with the legal codes concerning suicide, it is disallowed, today, for the state to restrict the high levels of risk involved in certain kinds of sports (e.g., mountain climbing). It counts as a given that, in every individual life, the freedom should be preserved to terminate sexual partnerships, membership in religious communities, and professional occupations—and that the abandoned positions be replaced, at a given moment and at will, with transitional arrangements. Our life in the broad present is dissolving, as Peter Sloterdijk first recognized, into more and more practice exercises.

After the oscillation—indeed, the leap—between the desire for collective life on our planet and the fading away of life's concreteness (which seems to undermine the first time and again), and after the second oscillation, which occurs when one gives the right to one's body over to the care of the state even while, at the same time, aggressively claiming to own it as a plaything, comes the third of the four oscillations that characterize life in our broad present. This force field also begins with the physical side of human existence, at least in part. It concerns a marked fluctuation that occurs in dealing with power. Here, I understand "power" as violence that has moved from the sphere of immediate action and effect into the realm of raw potential. "Violence" concerns human bodies that, by blocking or occupying space, offer resistance to other bodies. It is part of the process of modernization—some would say a part of every historical process that deserves to be called a civilizing process—to follow the general commandment that the immediacy of violence be transformed into power, which exists in reserve.

Since the middle of the twentieth century, it has become standard practice in the Western world not to show weapons publicly. Ever since state communism collapsed in Eastern Europe, in 1989, military parades have occurred only rarely on the international stage. For intellectuals and many international organizations, the death penalty has come to count as a symptom of barbarism, and every day the question becomes more pressing whether—except, perhaps, in extreme cases of self-defense—it is possible to identify situations in which the deployment of military force is justified. The proposal, made at the beginning of 2010 by German politicians, of not fighting the Taliban militarily, but instead offering 30,000 euros to all adherents who renounced their ideological convictions, may represent the culmination of the progressive elimination of military force as a political instrument.

Yet in this same present, and to a greater degree than ever before, people inflict violence on their own bodies unnecessarily and without a clear, practical motivation. Part—or, perhaps, the core—of the "general mobilization" we have already discussed is the general, impersonal obligation to always be in excellent physical "shape." This demand does not respect differences of age, and, consequently, the indefinite prolongation of youth has become a universal goal. Plastic surgery is the thriving trade of our time—and its operations are the most benign expression of the new physical self-reflexivity. Already, in adolescence, the pressure to adapt one's body to ideal images is experienced with such intensity that, among young women especially, it transforms into various eating disorders—that is to say, into long-term violence to one's own body. There are, moreover, piercings, tattoos, self-inflicted mutilations, and, finally, waves of suicide; those who are "their own victims" often associate (insofar as they can still speak at all) these activities with the yearning to ascertain the presence of their own bodies through pain.

Such forms of behavior, I believe, do not belong to the *micropouvoirs*—that is, the operations of power undertaken on the self—that Michel Foucault often discussed, especially in his later writings. Foucault was talking about a structurally similar figure of self-reflection: the internalization of socially established values to which one adapts one's "own," individual conduct. However, since no physical violence is actually manifest here, it is only possible to speak of a self-reflective function of power. These forms of behavior, which stand in sharp contrast to the elimination of violence from society and politics and cannot be reconciled with it, are cases in which power is wielded on the self—there is no authority that stands behind the activities in whose name they occur. If electronic media generate a self-enslaving obligation "to be available" that has made us a people of subjects without masters, then self-reflective violence represents a kind of dramatic intensification before which we stand helpless. The more self-evident and pressing the situation becomes to us, the more important it seems for our survival that we perform a leap into the dreams and illusions of the world as a place without violence or power.

The fourth and last oscillation of our broad present that I would like to discuss concerns the way we think. Electronic media, through their tendency to eliminate space from communication, have markedly increased the tempo with which the circulation of thoughts is effected. Since, in a broad present with an obstructed future, there is no place for thought that founds human action by aiming for goals, thinking may, today more than ever, have become synonymous with circulation—that is, a process of merely passing thoughts along. (For precisely this reason, perhaps, some of us experience "creativity" as the ability to intercept them.) Instead of conceiving projects or "edifices" of thought, our role in the system of knowledge-circulation resembles the part of an athlete playing "one-touch soccer." Instead of trying to keep the ball until making a decisive pass or a shot, players are supposed to kick the ball to a teammate moving freely in an uncovered position. The ball is supposed to circulate without interruption, undetained even for brief moments of rest. Like lead players, "master thinkers" also seem to disappear under these conditions.

On the other side of this fourth field of polar oscillation, it is precisely thought, as a praxis and dimension of existence, that has been claimed as a way to take distance from the existential acceleration fueled by "general mobilization"—indeed, to a certain degree, it even offers a certain potential for resistance.

Today the equation of "thinking" and "distinction" in Aristotle's works has received renewed attention inasmuch as the latter is understood not in terms of the difference between concepts, but as an intervention that occurs among the things-of-the-world. In the last few decades no philosopher viewed this matter with more passion than Jean-François Lyotard. Simply taking the necessary time, whether alone or in a group, to think without a practical goal in mind represented, for him, the ultimate possibility for "revolutionary" action remaining to intellectuals (whatever we may consider to be the stakes of the title *revolutionary*, which used to be a badge of honor).

Even more important, for me, are Lyotard's speculations about sex-specific modes of thought, which are suffused with particular experiences of embodiment and physical function—for example, his intuition that the specific intensity of feminine thought might have something to do with the specific intensity of physical suffering. Of course, the point is not to return to the suppositions of the master thinker who left us in 1998. Thinking is a point of reference in the oscillation that characterizes our broad present because in thought we can leap, from the feeling of acceleration and complexity that overwhelms us, to a decelerated enclave of calm.

*

The more, the more often—and, perhaps, even, the more willingly—I have let myself, in the past years, yield to the temptation to insist on presence and, in so doing, to describe and analyze individual phenomena in our present, the more I have encountered a reaction—which quickly transformed into an objection— that the almost aggressive pessimism of my diagnoses stands in conflict with the rather more optimistic (or, at any rate, friendly) undertone of what I say. For my part, I can see, both in what I have written and in my life, a growing pessimism coupled with occasional "optimism"—however, I do not see the contradiction between them.

The social and, so to speak, the cosmic conditions for this pessimism—with all their many effects—are obvious. They form the subject matter of the chapters in this book (without, for all that, being part of a program of *sounding* pessimistic). A complicating thought, which is just as simple as it is terrifying, overshadowed this scene not too long ago, and it has not left me. It occurred for the first time when I was reading the "Letter on Humanism," which Martin Heidegger wrote in the immediate aftermath of the Second World War. It can best be put as a rhetorical question: How can human beings ever assume, with certainty, that their cognitive and intellectual abilities will be enough to secure their continued existence as a species? Most cultures in history have lived under the existential premise that there exists cognitive symmetry—or even harmony—between "man," who is the product of development, and the universe that forms his surroundings (which he endeavors to understand). The insights that the natural sciences have afforded us in recent decades hardly encourage us to continue in this belief. But even if a better situation existed with respect to human intelligence, and even if the ecological future faced less dramatic prospects, we, as a species and as a community sharing a cosmic destiny, cannot proceed with certainty. This, however, is little more than a restatement of radical, "green" arguments, which nobody really needs to hear again.

Recently, my eldest son, who is a pilot in the German Air Force, spoke with remarkable professional matter-of-factness of a world war for resources. I would certainly escape it, and he possibly would, too. But his daughter—my granddaughter Clara—would not. The last part of what he said affected me profoundly—"it hit close to home," as one says, and in a more profound way than the abstractions of philosophical ethics ever could. All the same—apart from a somewhat vague "general experience"—it is not entirely clear why the life and potential suffering of my granddaughter gripped me in such a singularly intense way. At any rate, I can associate the intensity of my concern with the intensity of the joy I experienced when Clara recognized my face for the first time—with the joy between us when she sits on my lap and, together, we look at a picture book.

It is safe to say that all of us feel a special yearning for moments of presence in our broad present. I would not call it "optimism" that I try to find them—to grasp them and to be open to their fullness. Instead, it is a matter of the will-to-presence. To give it up—or to sacrifice it to the intellectual pseudo-obligation of permanent criticism—would really be asking too much.

NOTES

1. PRESENCE IN LANGUAGE OR PRESENCE ACHIEVED AGAINST LANGUAGE?

1. These premises are laid out and argued in much greater detail by my recent book, *Production of Presence: What Meaning Cannot Convey* (Stanford: Stanford University Press, 2003); German translation under the title *Diesseits der Hermeneutik. Die Produktion von Praesenz* (Frankfurt, 2004). Regarding a possible place for this reflection on presence in today's philosophical debates, see my essay "Diesseits des Sinns. Ueber eine neue Sehnsucht nach Substantialitaet," in *Merkur* 677/678 (2005): 749–760.
2. See, above all, his book *The Birth to Presence* (Stanford: Stanford University Press, 1993); some other contemporary examples for this tendency are mentioned and discussed in Gumbrecht, *Production of Presence*, pp. 57–64.
3. For a more fully developed version of this typology, see Gumbrecht, *Production of Presence*, pp. 78–86.
4. Hans Georg Gadamer, *Hermeneutik, Aesthetik, Praktische Philosophie*, ed. Carsten Dutt, 3. Auflage (Heidelberg: Universitätsverlag Winter, 2000), p. 63.
5. This description is based on my essay: "Rhythm and Meaning," in H. U. Gumbrecht and K. Ludwig Pfeiffer, eds., *Materialities of Communication* (Stanford: Stanford

University Press, 1994), pp. 170–186; original German version in *Materialitaet der Kommunikation* (Frankfurt, 1988), pp. 714–729.

6. See my analysis of some old high German charms ("The Charm of Charms") in David Wellbery, eds., *A New History of German Literature* (Cambridge: Harvard University Press, 2004), pp. 183–191.

7. *The Powers of Philology: Dynamics of Textual Scholarship* (Chicago: University of Chicago Press, 2003) German translation under the title "Die Macht der Philologie. Über einen verborgenen Impuls im wissenschaftlichen Umgang mit Texten" (Frankfurt: Suhrkamp, 2003).

8. Erwin Schroedinger, "Autobiographial Sketches," in *What Is Life?* (Cambridge: Cambridge University Press, 1992), pp. 165–187.

9. Karl Heinz Bohrer, *Plötzlichkeit. Zum Augenblick des ästhetischen Scheins* (Frankfurt: Suhrkamp, 1981) and *Der Abschied. Theorie der Trauer* (Frankfurt: Suhrkamp, 1996).

10. See Gumbrecht, *Production of Presence* (Stanford: Stanford University Press, 2003), pp. 65–78.

11. See the outlines for a history of this paradigm in my essay "Ausdruck," in Karlheinz Barck a.o. eds., *Ästhetische Grundbegriffe*, vol. 1 (Stuttgart: Metzler, 2000), pp. 416–431.

12. For such resonating voices, see the 2005 special issue of the magazine *Merkur* dedicated to new intellectual quests for Reality.

13. For more detailed descriptions focusing on the existential effects of new communication technologies, see my essay "Gators in the Bayoo: What We Have Lost in Disenchantment?" Forthcoming in Joshua Landy and Michael Saler, eds., *The Re-Enchantment of the World: Secular Magic in a Rational Age* (Berkeley: University of California Press, 2006).

2. A NEGATIVE ANTHROPOLOGY OF GLOBALIZATION

1. For more on hybridity, see, e.g., Homi Bhabha, *Location of Culture* (London: Routledge, 1995).

2. On globalization, see John Beynon and David Dunkerley, eds., *Globalization: The Reader* (New York: Routledge, 2000); Ulrich Broeckling, Susanne Krasmann, and Thomas Lemke, eds., *Glossar der Gegenwart* (Frankfurt: Suhrkamp, 2004); Gary M. Kroll and Richard H. Robbins, eds., *World in Motion: The Globalization and Environment Reader* (Lanham, MD: AltaMira, 2009); Frank J. Lechner and John Boli, *The Globalization Reader* (Malden, MA: Blackwell, 2000; Jonathan Michie, ed., *The Handbook of Globalization* (Cheltenham: Edward Elgar, 2003); James H. Mittelman, ed., *Globalization: Critical Reflections* (London: Lynne Rienner, 1996); Juergen Mittelstrass, "Focus—Global Science, the Future of Science: A Welcome Address." *European Review* 17 (2009): 463–468; Jochen Rack, "Bilder aus der globalisierten Welt," *Merkur* 723 (2009): 736–742; Paul W. Rhode and Gianni

Toniolo, eds., *The Global Economy in the 1990s: A Long-Run Perspective* (Cambridge: Cambridge University Press, 2006); J. Timmons Roberts and Amy Bellone Hite, eds., *The Globalization and Development Reader: Perspectives on Development and Global Change* (Malden, MA: Blackwell, 2007); Saskia Sassen, *Globalization and Its Discontents* (New York: New Press, 1998).

3. See Alfred Schütz and Thomas Luckmann, *The Structures of the Life-World* (Evanston, IL: Northwestern University Press, 1973); and Hans Ulrich Gumbrecht, *Production of Presence—What Meaning Cannot Convey* (Stanford: Stanford University Press, 2004).

4. For more, see chapter 2, Gumbrecht, *Production of Presence*.

5. See Hans Ulrich Gumbrecht, *In Praise of Athletic Beauty* (Cambridge: Harvard University Press, 2006).

6. Peter Sloterdijk, *You Must Change Your Life* (Cambridge: Polity, 2013).

7. See book on derivatives by Joseph Vogl, Das Gespenst des Kapitals, Berlin: Diaphanes, 2010).

8. Martin Heidegger, "Building Dwelling Thinking" (1951), in *Poetry, Language, Thought* (New York: Harper and Row, 1975), pp. 143–162.

9. See Robert Harrison, *Forests—the Shadow of Civilization* (Chicago: Chicago University Press, 1992), *The Dominion of the Dead* (Chicago: Chicago University Press, 2003), and *Gardens: An Esssay on the Human Condition* (Chicago: Chicago University Press, 2008).

10. Hannah Arendt, *The Human Condition* (Chicago: Chicago University Press, 1958).

3. STAGNATION

1. This process is described at length in chapter 2 of my book *Production of Presence: What Meaning Cannot Convey* (Stanford: Stanford University Pres, 2004), pp. 21–50, especially pp. 38ff.

2. Cf. the extensive account of this situation in my essay, "Die Gegenwart wird immer breiter," *Merkur* 629/630 (2001): 769–784.

3. *Rational Reenchantment* is the programmatic title—referring, negatively, to Max Weber—of a collection of essays edited by Joshua Landy and Michael Saller (Berkeley: University of Berkeley Press, 2008).

4. Cf. my "Bibliothek ohne Buch," *Frankfurter Allgemeine Zeitung*, March 19, 2008.

5. Cf. Gumbrecht, *Production of Presence*, pp. 80–86.

4. "LOST IN FOCUSED INTENSITY"

1. Quoted from my book *In Praise of Athletic Beauty* (Cambridge: Harvard University Press), pp. 50f. This text is the source for several historical facts and, above all, the

point of departure for some concepts and motifs that I will try to develop on the following pages.

2. For more evidence regarding this thesis, and a list of Heidegger references, see Hans Ulrich Gumbrecht, *Production of Presence: What Meaning Cannot Convey* (Stanford: Stanford University Press, 2004), pp. 64–78.

3. Martin Heidegger, *An Introduction to Metaphysics*, trans. Ralph Manheim (New Haven: Yale University Press, 1986), p. 1.

4. The second chapter of *In Praise of Athletic Beauty* presents more evidence for this view.

INDEX